BEYOND THE RANGES

BEYOND THE RANGES

An Autobiography

by

KENNETH SCOTT LATOURETTE

*Sterling Professor of Missions and Oriental History and
Fellow of Berkeley College, Emeritus, in
Yale University*

WILLIAM B. EERDMANS PUBLISHING COMPANY
GRAND RAPIDS, MICHIGAN

279 42

PREFACE

The title, *Beyond the Ranges*, with its reminiscence of Kipling's *The Explorer*, may seem a strange choice for an autobiography of one most of whose life has been spent in academic circles. Yet as the story unfolds, the appropriateness will become apparent. As, in my eighties, I look back across the years, I seem to see that, sometimes reluctantly, I have been breaking new trails. Again and again I have been on a frontier with others, but more than once mine began as a solitary exploration, and for me "a voice as bad as conscience" rang interminable changes on one everlasting whisper, day and night repeated thus: " 'Something hidden, go and find it; go and look beyond the ranges. Something lost beyond the ranges, lost and waiting for you, go.' " Occasionally others have followed the trails that I have sought to blaze. At times I have joined with companions in trudging along trails which those before me have marked out. Now and again a trail has not attracted others and has ended in an impasse. When the trail attracted others and led beyond "the edge of cultivation" into a "never, never country," an exciting new region, I can only be profoundly grateful that God "chose me for His whisper" and I can honestly say: "Anybody might have found it, but His whisper came to me."

What follows is an account of a particular life, the heredity and environment which shaped it, the choices which were made, often with agony and great uncertainty as to the outcome, and something of the results which followed. Some of the inner struggles are not given. That is partly because they are too intimate and concern no one but the author, but mainly because they have no special significance for the chief purpose of this little book. That purpose is to picture the setting of the early and formative years, the major stages of that life, and something of the individuals, movements, and institutions with which that life has been associated. Since in one way or another these have included much of the world of the first six decades of the twentieth century, those who read these pages will find in them not only a record of one man, but also something of the age in which his years were spent. Here is no *apologia pro vita mea*, but an attempt, so far as I am able, objectively to put down that record as though I were writing about someone else. Yet because of an obvious intimacy of knowledge which a biographer could not possess, it may be more revealing and informing than even the best of biographies could be.

CONTENTS

CHAPTER I

THE FAMILY BACKGROUND AND THE SETTING OF THE EARLY FORMATIVE YEARS

By family background and heredity, as I now see clearly, I was prepared to be a trail blazer and to go in the direction which the trails have mainly taken. In both my father's and my mother's family was a long tradition of adventuring on new and unmapped frontiers in response to "a voice as bad as conscience."

The first of my Latourette ancestors in America was Jean Latourette, from Osse in Bearne, on the extreme southwest edge of the French Pyrenees. On July 16, 1693, his marriage to Marie Mercereaux was recorded, under English law, in the French Church in New York City, presumably a reconfirmation of an earlier ceremony in France. Jean and Marie were Huguenots, refugees from the persecution instituted by Louis XIV. They came to New York City about 1685 in a ship which a storm had driven off its course. Whether they were Protestants by heredity is not known, but they obviously had left their native land for conscience' sake to adventure in what for them was an alien country. Jean took out citizenship in the colony, and in 1698 acquired land on Staten Island. There he built a house and was warden of St. Andrews Church. One of his descendants moved as a young man to Lodi, on the shore of Lake Seneca, New York, on what was then the frontier. There he married Hannah Hegeman. Hannah was of the Dutch stock which had been in America for several generations. She was deeply religious

9

and on being introduced to a stranger would ask: "Are you a Christian?" One of her sons, Lyman D. C. Latourette, was my father's father. By his own efforts he acquired an academy education, taught school, and in 1848 went by "covered wagon"—by the six months' journey which that adventure entailed—to Oregon. His first winter in Oregon he taught in a school in Forest Grove which was the predecessor of Tualatin Academy and Pacific University. In 1849 he was for a few months in the gold fields in California and acquired about seven thousand dollars in gold dust. Returning to Oregon, he hewed a farm out of the woods a few miles from Oregon City, reared a family of children, was the main pillar of the Baptist Church in that town, and taught a Sunday School class of young men. He had family worship as regularly as the sun rose.

Lyman D. C. Latourette married a daughter of Ezra Fisher and, after her death, her younger sister. Ezra Fisher was descended from Anthony Fisher, a Puritan, who came to Dedham, Massachusetts, in 1637, also responding to the voice of conscience to seek to serve God as he believed He wished in what was still a wilderness. Born and reared in a new settlement in Wendell, in the western part of the state, Ezra Fisher went to the infant Amherst College, founded to prepare young men for the ministry. He had been converted in his late teens and was headed for that profession. Somewhere along the line his forebears had departed from the Congregational establishment. His father was one of the organizers of the Baptist Church in Wendell. Ezra Fisher married Lucy Taft, a neighbor, to whom he had been long engaged. Together they served Baptist churches in Vermont, at that time not far removed from the frontier. In their early thirties, impressed with the religious needs of the Mississippi Valley, then being settled, they sought appointment under the recently organized American Baptist Home Mission Society. They served in raw new towns in Indiana, Illinois, and Iowa. In 1845, choosing between newer frontiers in Texas and Oregon, with another Baptist minister, Hezekiah Johnson, and the latter's family, they made the months-long trip by ox team to the vast region in the Pacific Northwest which was still under the joint occupancy of Great Britain and the United States. The two families were the first representatives of the American Baptist Home Mission Society on the West Coast. As he had done in Indiana, so also in Oregon, Ezra Fisher led in the first efforts to establish higher education under Baptist auspices.

My mother's father was John Tucker Scott. In him, as in the Latourettes and the Fishers, the lure of the frontier and religious conviction were strong. Soon after the American Revolution his grandfather had followed the Wilderness Trail through the Cumberland Gap and had become one of the hardy pioneers in Kentucky. There John Tucker Scott was born. When he was about fourteen, his father, from a prosperous, slave-holding family, but opposed to slavery, moved to free territory on "the edge of cultivation" in Central Illinois. His home was deeply religious. John Tucker's younger sister, Rhoda, for whom my mother was named, educated in one of the "female seminaries" founded in Illinois by earnest Christians, became the wife of a clergyman who went as a missionary to Turkey under the American Board of Commissioners for Foreign Missions. When John Tucker Scott established his home, it became a center of hospitality to travelling ministers. Throughout his life family worship was part of the daily routine. In 1852, when he was forty-three, John Tucker Scott, responding to the urge that had moved his grandfather and father, sold his holdings and with his wife and eight children started on the half-year expedition to Oregon. He had obtained all the information possible and had made careful preparations, but the journey proved more exacting than he had anticipated. He and his party travelled about fifteen miles a day and each twenty-four hours counted ten or more new-made graves. On the way his wife and youngest child died. In the party was my mother's mother, Ruth Eckler, and her husband. Ruth Eckler was also of hardy pioneer stock and was born in Kentucky. She was of Pennsylvania "Dutch" (German) and Virginia Huguenot stock. As a girl she had joined the "Christian" denomination which had sprung from the awakening led by Barton W. Stone, and throughout her life maintained that connection. Just as they were about to reach their destination, her husband died, leaving her with a small son. John Tucker Scott befriended her, and within a few months they were married.

My father, Dewitt Clinton Latourette, was born and reared on his father's farm near Oregon City. Coming from that devout home, it was natural that in his childhood he awoke one morning in his bed in the log cabin with the assurance that he had been born anew. He said nothing about it, but his grandmother, Hannah Hegeman, who was living in the home, observed the quiet joy that had come and remarked: "Clinton is a converted boy." From that experience, ripened with years, he never departed. When he was in his teens, his father sent him to Forest Grove, to Pacific University and the preparatory department, Tualatin Academy. Pacific University was founded by New England Congregationalists who with heroism and devotion sought to establish in that new country an institution which would embody the best of the Christian colleges from which they came. But its designation, Pacific University, embodied a dream which was not fully realized. It was the first college to grant degrees in the United States west of the Rockies. Although with limited physical resources, it was progressive educationally and gave as good a college education as could be obtained anywhere in the country at the time.

While in college my father met my mother, Rhoda Ellen Scott. She had been born near the later Olympia, Washington, when her father, uncles, and brother were fighting what proved to be the last war with the Indians on Puget Sound. As an infant she was taken by her mother, for protection, to a neighboring blockhouse. Her

father and mother later made their home in Forest
Grove. There she was reared, and as she reached adoles-
cence sang and played the organ in the Congregational
church which was the center of the religious life of both
the village and the college. She and my father were
classmates. From Pacific University they each received
their B. A. and M. A.

After graduation my father taught for two years in
what was hopefully named McMinnville College (later
Linfield), but which then served the village as a common
school and academy. It had its roots in what Ezra Fisher
had begun in Oregon City. Then, living on his savings, he
"read law" with two deacons of the Oregon City Baptist
Church. In 1882 he was "admitted to the bar." One of the
deacons was the son of the Hezekiah Johnson with whom
Ezra Fisher had "crossed the plains." While waiting for
my father, my mother taught Latin in Seattle, in what
was ambitiously called the University of Washington, and
then in Forest Grove. Throughout the rest of his long life
my father "practised law" in Oregon City. For nearly fifty
years it was as a partner with his first cousin, Charles D.
Latourette. He was also president of the bank which he
and his partner founded and owned. It was in Oregon
City, on August 9, 1884, that I was born as the first child
of my father and mother.

From what I have thus far said, something of the
background out of which I came must be apparent. Obviously in my childhood and youth I was only slightly aware
of it. For generations trail blazing had been in the blood
of my forebears. Much, but not all of it, had come from
profound Christian conviction and had been sustained by
Christian faith. As I look back across the decades I am
aware of additional factors. Among them are the gift of
verbal memory and the urge to write which I now realize
came from the Scott ancestry. My mother's older half-
brother, Harvey W. Scott, had both to a much greater
degree than I. He could quote pages of poetry, in English and Latin. He was fourteen when, with his fa-

ther, he arrived in Oregon. Through gruelling physical labor under the rough conditions on the frontier he had supported himself, with his earnings helped his father, and obtained an education. He was the first graduate of Pacific University, and thus was the first on the Pacific Coast of the United States to be given an academic degree. For more than forty years he was editor of *The Morning Oregonian* of Portland. He made it the leading newspaper of the Pacific Northwest. By his editorials on religion, politics, literature, history, and education he was outstanding in shaping the thought of that vast region. He read prodigiously in the subjects with which he dealt and accumulated a large library which he knew thoroughly. I saw little of him and not until middle life did I read much that he had written. I could not either consciously or unconsciously have been influenced by him. My mother had something of the same verbal memory, was deeply interested in literature, geography, and music—traits which came from the Scott side of her parentage—and much that she had rubbed off on me. In addition, from both my father and mother, and especially my mother, came an idealization of the academic life. They spoke frequently of their college days, of the friendships formed there, and of their debt to their teachers. In that frontier college, struggling and, from the standpoint of the twentieth century, with meager physical equipment, the faculty lived sacrificially, and gave themselves unstintedly to their students in mental discipline and in personal friendship, contagious examples of cultivated Christian character. The home in which I was reared was an embodiment of Christian faith and culture. My parents' marriage was eminently successful. My mother often suffered from ill health, but it seldom kept her from being an unusually efficient homemaker. My father had a superb physique and was invariably cheerful and hopeful. He was successful in his business and profession and provided the home with all the comforts needed for the rearing of his children. Because of their college education, both parents had built up a well-stocked library with predominantly Victorian writers. It contained a full set of Dickens, George Eliot, Bulwer Lytton, Tennyson, and selections from other authors. To them as a lad I added the Waverly novels. It also had an excellent encyclopedia, atlases, and Hubert Howe Bancroft's voluminous histories of the West Coast and Southwestern States and Mexico. In my boyhood the town had no public library and the school libraries, though well selected, were small. As a bookish lad I read most of what was in the home, especially of history and fiction, and added or borrowed from my chums such books as G. A. Henty's historical novels for boys and Cooper's novels. In my teens I was thrilled by James Bryce's essay on *The Holy Roman Empire*. I also owned and read Prescott's *Conquest of Mexico* and *Conquest of Peru*.

My father and mother built their home around the Christian faith. They unfailingly had morning family worship with Scripture reading, hymns, and prayer. As we children grew older the memorization of verses and chapters of the Bible was added and we were encouraged to offer prayer and play the piano for hymns. My father became a life-deacon. Both he and my mother taught Sunday School classes through most of their married life. For several years they conducted a mission Sunday School in a nearby suburb. Attendance at church and Sunday School was not required, but it was part of the family pattern which we children accepted as a matter of course. As we reached our teens we were encouraged to make a formal commitment to Christ, and through baptism (by immersion, for the church was Baptist) to make public profession of our faith and become church members. The ethical and social standards were those customary in Evangelical circles of the day, but no compulsion was employed. My father did not use tobacco or alcohol, but took no promise to abstain and when I as a child signed the total abstinence pledge he did not forbid it but clearly felt it to be unwise. We did not dance, go to the theater, or use the traditional playing cards. But we had family games—cards in the form of *Authors* (which made us familiar with the names of the better writers in English), checkers, croquet, and dominoes—and my father often read aloud to us, usually from *The Youth's Companion*, which was then in thousands of American homes. We children were early encouraged in thrift and work. As recreation my father kept cows, chickens, and a horse on one of the two blocks which he owned in town. I distributed the surplus milk, collected the bills, drove the cows to pasture, and worked summers on farms—one which my grandfather had made and which my father supervised after his father's death, and one which my father bought when it was still in timber, had cleared and brought under cultivation.

When I was a lad Oregon City was small. It was the oldest town in the state, for it was located at "the Falls of the Willamette," where that river tumbled over a fifty-foot cliff, a source of water-power and, in the days of water-transportation, a trans-shipping point from the lower to the upper reaches of that stream. It had been the first territorial capital in the Pacific Northwest, in it had been published the first newspaper on the West Coast, it was usually regarded as the end of the Oregon Trail, and in it were the oldest Protestant church and the oldest Masonic lodge west of the Rockies. But it was too far up the river to be a port for ocean-going ships—which Portland, about fifteen miles farther down the Willamette early became—political maneuvers placed the capital and various state institutions elsewhere, and it depended for its livelihood upon the fact that it was the county-seat and on the mills which utilized its water-power.

Naturally my boyhood centered around the family, the church, and the public schools. Much of the family's social as well as its religious life was in the local Baptist Church. That church is now the oldest existing Baptist Church west of the Rockies, for slightly earlier churches, being rural, have long since died. In my boyhood it was in the Moody tradition, with emphasis upon John 3:16 as the best brief summary of the Gospel, with the Moody and Sankey hymns in the Sunday School (more dignified, but still Evangelical hymns were used in the morning worship service), and from time to time with special evangelistic services by visiting preachers. I was partly reared in the Congregational Church which some of my chums attended. In my early teens I went for several months to even-song in the Episcopal Church, where one of my father's cousins was senior warden, and ever since have prized the Book of Common Prayer. On the same block with the Baptist Church was the Roman Catholic Church, but it was not until my thirties that I became a close friend of the priest who had been its pastor from my earliest recollection. Incidentally, Oregon City had been made the head of the second Roman Catholic archdiocese in the United States, with Baltimore the first. I attended the public schools. When I was not quite sixteen I graduated from the high school. Until my class that school had only two years above the eighth grade. We were given three years, but the following year the course was again reduced to two years.

Community life was simple but varied. Not until my teens were there any organized athletics. They were then in the local YMCA, where I played basketball. We boys taught one another swimming. While learning, I was nearly drowned and a few years later my younger brother was drowned in the same spot. Morally, we lads were not aware of irregularities, but I later learned that in a local club gambling was a recreation, and that some of the local physicians were alcoholics and had irregular relations with women. Saloons were wide open, and in them many of the laborers in the mills cashed their pay checks and spent much of the proceeds. A crude form of atheism was prevalent among the poorly educated, and agnosticism and a more rationalized scepticism characterized many in professional and business circles. This I knew, but it did not then trouble me. In later years I was affected by the departure of Harvey Scott and the more intellectual of my mother's half-sisters from their inherited faith. Here was an honest and intelligent questioning of basic Christian convictions which eventually I had to face.

Since on my graduation from high school I was still very young and not sufficiently mature for college, my father suggested that I stay out of school for a year. He employed me in the bank of which he was president and part of the time I kept the books in his law office, for the two were closely related and in the same building. The experience in business has proved valuable. At the same time I read some Latin with my mother—chiefly Cicero's *Orations* and Virgil's *Aeneid*.

In September, 1901, I enrolled as a sophomore in McMinnville (later Linfield) College. The decision was by my parents. Pacific University, their *alma mater*, would have seemed to be the natural choice, partly because of their connection and partly because academically it was superior to McMinnville and equal to any institution on the West Coast of that day. However, denominational and family reasons were determinative. McMinnville College was Baptist in affiliation, its foundations went back to Ezra Fisher, my father had taught there, was a trustee and invested its funds, and his step-mother, who, as I have said, was his aunt and whom I regarded as my grandmother, made her home there to educate her children, his half-brothers and sisters. I had often visited there and knew the faculty. By 1901 my grandmother had moved to Portland, but her youngest child, only a few months older than I and much like a sister to me, was still in college, in my class. My father's older brother was field agent for the college. I have sometimes wondered what my future would have been had I gone to Pacific University. The probabilities are that I would not have been a missionary. As will be apparent, a combination of circumstances at McMinnville which probably would not have developed at Pacific exposed me forcibly to the world mission.

Although McMinnville granted degrees, by later standards it was only a junior college—as was seen by the fact that I entered in sophomore year and by taking a little extra work graduated in three years. Life was very simple. During none of my years there did the student body number as many as two hundred. More of them were in the preparatory department, in a business department, and taking music than were candidates for degrees. The physical plant was limited. The one substantial building, of brick, in four stories, had been erected twenty years earlier on an ample campus. That building housed the offices, classrooms, chapel, laboratories, printing plant, dining hall, and library, and some of the staff. In addition were an observatory and a poorly equipped frame gymnasium. The endowment was about fifty thousand dollars and the debt, most of which my father carried, was not far from that sum. Tuition was forty-five dollars a year with a ten percent discount if paid in advance. The core of the faculty were able and self-sacrificing and carried incredible teaching loads. None had a Ph. D., and only two or three a degree above a B. A. They remained with the college because they believed in it as a Christian institution and served on mere pittances which were frequently in arrears. They were paid in warrants which my father often cashed and carried until the college could redeem them—sometimes only after several years. The long-time dean, a graduate of Colgate, supplemented his salary by working nights and Saturdays in a local insurance company. Several not only gave themselves devotedly to the students in classroom and laboratory, but as well shared in their social life and entertained them in their homes.

The strongest departments were the natural sciences. Latin, Greek, French, and German were taught, but almost no history. Some English was included, and a little philosophy and economics. Yet I have often said that the best teaching was certainly as good, and perhaps better, than the best I later had at Yale, and the worst teaching was not as bad as the worst that I had at Yale.

Since I did not expect ever to have use for Greek, I took none of it and so was a candidate for the Bachelor of Science. So far as that could be done, I majored in the sciences and took all of the introductory and some of the advanced courses. I had no history—indeed I had had almost none in high school—and had only one course in English composition and literature, and that in my first year. No courses in religion were given, but daily chapel was required.

College life had a great fascination for me and I entered in all phases of it except athletics. Without any prohibiting rules, the campus knew little smoking or card playing, no alcohol, and no dancing. Most of the students came from homes where these were tabooed and no requests were made for them. But many parties were held, formal and informal. Relations between the sexes were wholesome and a normal part of college life. Many marriages came out of the friendships and I recall only one that ended in divorce. I sang in the glee club and in one of the better musical comedies of the period. For two years I led the debating team—my last year to victory in the intercollegiate league. I was active in student body affairs, was president of the literary society, and entered —unsuccessfully—at least one oratorical contest. Prohibition sentiment was high, and I was a member of both the local and the state intercollegiate organizations for its promotion. Fraternities did not exist, but for about half my college course I was a member to the nearest approach to one—what was called the "bachelors' shack." A few of the men, five my first year and six my junior and the first part of my senior year, were living together to cut expenses. We rented a four-room house—for two dollars a month—did our own cooking, except for bread which we hired a woman to bake, picked our winter supply of apples on shares, and did our own laundry except our starched collars. The cost, including rent, light, heat, food, and water, was one dollar a week per man. We had an uproarious time. I entered into the company, not of financial necessity, but because I enjoyed the men and the fun. When I would write home about our exploits, my mother, an impeccable housekeeper, horrified, would ask my father to command me to leave the group, but he would laugh and say: "The boy is having a good time. Let him alone." Yet we did much studying and held some of the most important student offices. One of our number won the state intercollegiate oratorical contest. My closest friend, Charles Rutherford, nine years my senior, was for more than thirty years a faithful missionary in India. I graduated as the valedictorian of my class. The first six months and the last six months at McMinnville I roomed with private families and in the last six months had my meals in the college dining hall.

What proved determinative in the later course of my life was my share in the religious life of the college. For my three years I taught a Sunday School class of boys not much younger than I in the local Baptist Church, which was closely affiliated with the college. At the end of my first year I was elected president of the college's Young Men's Christian Association and held the office during my junior and senior years. At that time the student YMCAs were only about twenty-five years old. They were the one intercollegiate Christian organization of students in North America. They were warmly evangelistic and stressed Bible study. They held summer conferences. The first in the Pacific Northwest was at Gearhart, on a beach on the Pacific, about twelve miles south of the mouth of the Columbia River. It was at the close of my junior year. I attended, with Charles Rutherford. At that time I began a custom, made a decision, and faced an issue which were to shape the future course of my life. The custom was what was then known as "the morning watch." It meant fifteen minutes to an hour of private Bible reading and prayer. I remember on the first morning going alone into the woods and as I prayed nothing but silence seemed to answer. Yet I have maintained the custom over the more than sixty years which have followed, and during much of the time God has become increasingly real as a faithful companion and guide. Questions later came, of which I will speak in due course. The decision was to ask, in planning my future life, not what I would like to do, but what God would have me do. The issue was given poignancy by the presentation of foreign missions. The Student Volunteer Movement for Foreign Missions was then less than twenty years old. Membership involved signing the "declaration": "It is my purpose, if God permit, to become a foreign missionary." The "watchword" was "the evangelization of the world in this generation." By that was meant, not the conversion of the world in this generation, but the presentation of the Gospel to all, leaving to each hearer acceptance or rejection. A pamphlet by Robert E. Speer, whom in later years I came to know as an older and dear friend, entitled *What Constitutes a Missionary Call?* put it substantially as follows: "If you are a Christian, the burden of proof rests upon you to show why you should not become a foreign missionary." The challenge was stated clearly: in the United States all have the opportunity to hear the Gospel; in Asia, Africa, and many other areas, millions have not so much as heard the name of Christ; therefore, if you are a Christian, unless some clear obligation stands in the way, you should become a foreign missionary with your objective a share in fulfilling that watchword. I had not the remotest desire to become a foreign missionary. I had never even thought of becoming a clergyman. As long as I could remember, I had expected to follow my father and become a lawyer and banker in Oregon City. But, with my background, I could not escape the issue. During all the following year I struggled with it. A basic question was whether I did not owe it to my father to be with him in his profession. I had had two brothers, but one died in infancy and the other was drowned in the summer between my junior and senior years. Was it not therefore my duty to see my father through his declining years—although he then was not fifty! But the words kept ringing in my ears: "He that loves father and mother more than me is not worthy of me": "If anyone comes to me and does not hate his own father and mother and wife and children and brothers and sisters, yes, and even his own life, he cannot be my disciple." During the next Gearhart Conference—at the end of my senior year—I struggled with the problem with great agony. Finally, at the end of the conference, alone, I signed the "declaration." In doing so I felt as though I had signed my death warrant. The act was from a sheer sense of duty. My father was disappointed, but only once hinted at it. He did everything he could to help me prepare to fulfill that purpose.

Since at my graduation from McMinnville I was not quite twenty, my father thought that before I went on for more academic work I should have another year in business. Accordingly, I spent the next fifteen months at home working in one of the firms in which he was part owner, an abstract and trust company. During the year I learned to make abstracts of title. In addition, I was president of the young people's society in my church, taught a boys' Sunday School class and a Bible class in the local YMCA, and was president of the high school alumni association. I wished to go East for more college work and applied for advanced standing in Harvard, Princeton, Williams, Brown, and Yale. I knew so little about Yale that my first letter was addressed to "Yale University, Hartford, Connecticut." All but Yale admitted me to junior year. At that time the dean of Yale College, Henry Parks Wright, enrolled about twenty graduates of other colleges in senior year. His office wrote me that if I would pass entrance examinations in physics, economics, and Greek I would be among that number. I had had physics and economics, and they presented no problem. But I had had no Greek. My father and mother had taken it in college and still had their introductory texts, but had forgotten so much of it they could not help me. Equipped with their texts and without a tutor, I learned enough Greek grammar to read the *Anabasis*. I studied Greek at odd moments, at meal hours, and while walking to and from work. In the spring of 1905 I passed the Yale entrance examinations in the assigned subjects. On the side I completed an advanced correspondence course in the Old Testament offered by the international organization of the YMCA and was given credit based on an examination.

CHAPTER II

THE STUDENT YEARS IN YALE

In September, 1905, I arrived in New Haven, knowing almost nothing more about Yale than its name. Two lawyers in Oregon City were Yale graduates, but I had not consulted them. Indeed, although I was acquainted with them, I was not aware of their Yale connection. A cousin was in the junior class, but we had not seen each other since childhood. He did not look me up and I did not call on him for several weeks. With my YMCA background, I went at once to Dwight Hall, the building of the Yale YMCA, and began an association which has continued through the years.

Although I was not then aware of it, from the standpoint of my background Yale proved to be a much better place for me than would any of the other Eastern institutions to which I had applied. I later found that the YMCA in Yale was widely regarded as the strongest student association in the country. Yale itself had a warm Evangelical tradition which extended well back into the eighteenth century. Jonathan Edwards was an alumnus and for a time had been on the faculty. In the fore part of the nineteenth century the religious life had again and again been quickened by awakenings. In the last quarter of the nineteenth century Moody and Drummond had had a profound effect on the student body. At the student summer conferences at Northfield which were led by Moody and after the latter's death by John R. Mott, in the Moody tradition, Yale long had the largest delegation. Although only a minority of the student body were directly involved, Yale was a major center of interest in the Student Volunteer Movement. Several of the graduates of the 1890's had gone as missionaries to China, and in 1901, only four years before I came to Yale, a few of the recent graduates who were planning to be missionaries organized what became the Yale Foreign Missionary Society through which Yale men, supported by Yale friends, began as a group a mission in China. In common with several Eastern colleges, attendance was required at daily and Sunday chapel services. During my student years no complaint was raised against the custom. Indeed, my class voted overwhelmingly for its continuation. Immediately after Sunday chapel each of the four classes had a prayer meeting in Dwight Hall, led by members of the class. Attendance declined from freshman year onwards, but every Sunday in term time saw at least a faithful few, of whom I quickly became one, who in testimony and prayer maintained a warm fellowship. In Dwight Hall was also the "Semi-circular Room," where small groups met for prayer and where what was known as "the Student Volunteer Band," composed of those who were headed for foreign missions, met, usually weekly. Each Wednesday evening classes for Bible study gathered, one for each of the four classes. For many years undergraduates conducted the Bethany Sunday School not far from the campus in a small building it owned in a low income neighborhood. Occasionally I went and talked to the children. My first Sunday in New Haven I went to Calvary Baptist Church, the church of that denomination closest to the campus. I was deeply touched when a layman, a skilled mechanic, asked me to his home for dinner. That began a friendship with members of his family which continued through the years. I retained my membership in the church in Oregon City in which I had been reared, but in Calvary Baptist Church I soon began to teach a Sunday School class of boys not quite in their teens, and continued it through my four years. Because of my connection with the YMCA in Oregon City, I early sought out the New Haven YMCA. There I taught a Bible class for men, but because of involvements on the campus I did not continue it beyond the first year. Early in that first year I became acquainted with some in the freshman class, for they, like myself, were entering Yale. Among them I was privileged to form some close friendships, several of which were continued through their lifetime—for I am almost the only survivor of the circle whom I knew best.

Having come as a senior, when most of my class had been in Yale for three years and had formed their friendships, I had few intimates among them. I came to know the men who had, as I, entered in senior year. Among them one, Fulton Ferguson, was my roommate for my last three student years. He was in New Haven when I returned on the faculty. He and I have continued the friendship and I have become almost a part of his family. However, a few who had been with the class from the beginning of freshman year became close friends. Chief among them was John Magee. He came from a wealthy and socially prominent Pittsburgh family, but did not allow that background to keep him from those of quite different rearing. My class voted him to be its "most admired" member. He was headed for missions, was President of Dwight Hall, and after graduation was two years its resident secretary. He later was many years in China. After returning to this country he became chaplain to the Episcopal students in Yale, and we confirmed the friendship which had never lapsed.

One member of the class especially interested me. He was a warmhearted Irishman with whom I shared a table in Commons and one of my classes. Before I arrived he had become notorious for his flouting of most of the moral conventions. He drank heavily, had irregular relations with women, and most of the class, disgusted, had written him off. Because of poor grades he failed to graduate and his father disowned him. Toward the end of the

year I asked him why he did not stop his headlong
course, saying that he knew as well as I what it would
lead to. To my surprise he said that he would. Then, at
my suggestion, he gave me his hand on it. Somewhat to
the embarrassment of us both I told him that I would
remember him in prayer. I am glad to recall that we both
kept our word. At our triennial reunion he came and attached himself to me, for he knew that in my company
he would do no drinking. He later married a girl who
knew all about him, but loved him and believed in him.
He died early, probably as a result of his college dissipa-
tion.

One friendship begun in my senior year, which had as
great an effect on me as any formed at Yale, was with
Henry Burt Wright, of the class of 1898 and so about
eight years older than I. Henry Wright was the son of the
Dean of Yale College. Always of upright life, while an
undergraduate he made a conscious and revolutionary
commitment at a Northfield Conference as a result of an
appeal by Moody for a decision for Christ. In his senior
year he was President of Dwight Hall, and remained on as
resident secretary while doing graduate work in ancient
history. After taking his Ph. D. in that field, he became a
member of the faculty of Yale College. His chief concern
was for individuals. He taught a freshman Bible class in
the life of Christ, for to him Christ was central. He won
many a man to Christ, some of them students, some
adults, others rough lads in Oakham, the Massachusetts
village where his father had been reared and where the
family spent its summers. He was the most indefatigable
personal evangelist I have ever known. He gathered
about him a group, mostly of students who shared his
commitment to Christ, which met weekly and with whom
he revealed his deepest purposes and his faith. I became
a member of the group, as I recall it late in my first year,
and remained in it through my graduate school years. It
was chiefly that experience which has led me throughout
my teaching years to gather similar groups. When,

in my emeritus years, I was relieved of teaching and administration, as will appear later, I multiplied the groups until they numbered four—three meeting weekly by my fireside in the Divinity School and one in my office in Berkeley College, where I have been a Fellow.

In my election of courses I made choices which, in retrospect, I realize determined much of my future career and initiated one phase of my path-breaking. Those entering in senior year were not bound by requirements. We were permitted to elect any subjects to which we were attracted. Because in McMinnville I had majored in the natural sciences, I sought to fill the gaps which existed. Since I thought that in preparation for foreign missions I would need to go to a divinity school, I took Greek. There I ran into a barrier. The entering freshmen all had had more Greek than I. They had read the *Iliad* and so had been introduced to Homer. I went to the head teacher of Greek, Thomas Day Seymour, and told him of my predicament. Because in my entrance examination in Greek I had made a good grade, he admitted me to his division, promising not to call on me until I had become familiar with Greek scansion. I found myself in the section with the ablest freshmen, including some who became my closest friends. In the class was Harvey Bundy, charming and brilliant, later to be father of McGeorge and William Bundy, who in their maturity were prominent in the national government. I prize the memory of the course, chiefly because Seymour was an outstanding specialist in Homer and made the *Odyssey* come alive. We also read Plato's *Apology* and the *Phaedo*, but purely as a grammatical exercise with no attention to the issues with which they deal, and selections from Herodotus, similarly with no inkling of the light which they shed on the history which they record. Having had no philosophy except the traditional logic, I elected a course in epistemology. The lecturing was mediocre, but one of the required texts was excellent. Having had no history in McMinnville and very little in high school, I

majored in history and took honors in it. An excellent
course in economic history taught me the method of
note-taking in reading which I have ever since employed.
A course in American history from the Revolution to the
Civil War introduced me to historical method and to an
objective view of the period which disabused me of some
of the hyperpatriotic views which I had acquired from
popular history. Another on the period of the Reformation
and the Thirty Years' War was excellent for its clear and
orderly narrative. Since I was headed for foreign missions, although as yet with no clear idea of the country to
which to go, I chose the basic course which dealt with
regions outside Europe and the United States. That was a
comprehensive survey of the history of the Far East,
from India through China and Japan. The instructor was
Frederick Wells Williams, Assistant Professor of Oriental History. He was the son of Samuel Wells Williams, the
most eminent American sinologist of the nineteenth century, in his later years after long residence in China
Professor of Chinese in Yale, the earliest post of that kind
in any American university. Frederick Wells Williams
had helped his father in the extensive revision of *The
Middle Kingdom*, in its day the standard book in English
on Chinese history.

During the initial year at Yale I was deeply indebted to
Dean Wright. As with many students, he took a kindly
interest in me. At his suggestion I strove to achieve an
academic record which would entitle me to election in
Phi Beta Kappa—of which I had not been aware before
coming to Yale. Due largely to his counsel, I was elected
at the close of senior year.

Knowing nothing of fraternities when I entered Yale, I
was completely unfamiliar with the social hierarchy pe-
culiar to the college and soon learned that the elections
from my class had already been made. However, I was
asked into Alpha Chi Rho, a fraternity only recently
founded and Christian in its announced purpose. It was
outside the Yale society structure and not until my facul-

ty days did it gain recognition as a "junior fraternity." But in it I made several friends whom I learned greatly to value.

A major decision of senior year determined my future career. By spring of that year I was asked to prepare to join the staff of Yale-in-China. That invitation seemed to me to fulfill my purpose to be a missionary and through a channel which would give me full opportunity to utilize my major but as yet dimly discerned gifts. As I have said, from childhood I had been nurtured in a tradition established by dedicated Christian college teachers. In McMinnville and the year before coming to Yale a deep concern for boys younger than myself had been awakened, with a desire to lead them into the Christian faith and to help them grow in it. At the same time an interest in scholarship was beginning to develop—although I was not yet fully aware of it. Therefore I leaped to the invitation and decided to enter the Yale Graduate School to prepare for Yale-in-China through acquiring a Ph. D. Fortunately the Graduate School awarded me a fellowship which covered about half the expense and which was renewed during the remaining years at Yale.

The three years in the Graduate School were given to preparation for Yale-in-China and to Dwight Hall. The former entailed a Ph. D. I debated between seeking it in economics, geology, or history, for I was interested in all three subjects. Indeed, I took a course in field geology to supplement an introductory course in the subject in McMinnville. However, because I had majored in history in my senior year, and because of the interest then developed, I chose history. That was also because, in view of that major, I could obtain a Ph. D. in history more quickly than in any other subject. I took almost all the courses in history offered in the Graduate School. Among them was an introductory course in church history, which, although in the Divinity School, was given credit in the Graduate School. The instructor was Williston Walker, who in addition to being an outstanding scholar

was a superb lecturer. The chairman of the history department was George Burton Adams. He was a specialist
in English constitutional history, President of the American Historical Association, a clear, orderly lecturer, and
thoroughly competent in his seminars on feudalism and
the *curia regis*. The course in method was given by Edward Gaylord Bourne and proved to be the best teaching
that I had at Yale. I elected courses in ancient history,
Latin America, the economic history of the United States,
a seminar in American history, and audited a course by
Andrew W. Wheeler, who had held the first chair of
history in Yale and, although emeritus, was still lecturing
in his favorite subject, "Modern European History,"
which covered the years from 1815 to 1870. Since I was
going to China, I took two courses in Far Eastern history,
which, with the one I had had in senior year, were the
only ones offered in Yale. One was on the history of
Japan, by K. Asakawa, a brilliant Japanese scholar then at
the beginning of his career, and the other on the history
and culture of China, given by Frederick Wells
Williams.

For my dissertation I chose *The History of the Early
Relations between the United States and China,
1784-1844*. It was done under the direction of Professor
Williams. He proved to be a valued friend, for he was as
well Chairman of the Executive Committee of Yale-in-
China, and I spent many hours in his spacious library on
China and in his hospitable home. While doing my dissertation, the zest for research and writing awakened
which, as I have suggested, was latent in my Scott ancestry. I included in my subject every aspect of the first sixty
years of the contact of the United States with China—
commerce, diplomacy, and missions. The comprehen-
siveness of scope was unconsciously typical of most of my
later writings—an attempt to place the subject in its
setting and to cover all its phases. I examined the pertinent sources in printed books, manuscript government
documents, ships logs, and missionary archives from

Washington to Boston and Salem. No one had ever covered the subject, or, indeed, has since covered it as comprehensively and fully. Here I began breaking trail, venturing in the role of an explorer. The dissertation, published in 1917, has been twice reproduced (without asking my permission). I have seen the editions advertised but have never been given copies and have not purchased them.

Outside the field of strict history, but bearing on my projected life in China, I took a course in colonization. It was given by Albert G. Keller, the successor of William G. Sumner. The latter became emeritus during my student days.

Dwight Hall claimed much of my time. There my energies were directed chiefly to organizing and promoting Bible study among undergraduates and presenting to undergraduates the challenge of foreign missions.

During my senior year a new plan of voluntary Bible study by undergraduates was projected. The basic principle was to have Bible groups led by classmates. The leaders would be prepared in a normal class. The plan was to begin with the class of 1909, with whom I had entered Yale. I was asked to lead the normal class. Already outstanding in 1909 were several men who were known for their Christian commitment. The class numbered about 350. Approximately twenty leaders were chosen. They met, each selected the men whom he wished in his group, every man in the class was asked, and most accepted. I met the leaders each week. We had as our subject the life and teachings of Jesus. Each day the leaders gathered in Dwight Hall briefly for prayer. Eventually we asked in not only the leaders but also all in the class who shared a full commitment to Christ. The normal class met once a week. As 1909 moved into junior and senior year they went on with the groups, but I became responsible for the incoming sophomores, the class of 1910. That class did not have as many earnest Christians as 1909, but about twenty agreed to act as leaders. In the spring of freshman year we canvassed the entire class and the majority promised to come into one of the groups. In that class was Robert A. Taft, son of President Taft and later a distinguished United States Senator. He declined to lead a group, but agreed to see each leader every week and get a record of the attendance. Toward the end of the year the leaders presented me a Bible inscribed by Taft and signed by all of them. As 1910 became juniors and seniors their groups continued and I took the normal class of the incoming sophomores of 1911. That was in my last year in the Graduate School. We also extended the system into the Sheffield Scientific School, which was then distinct from Yale College. In my final year I was made Bible study secretary of Dwight Hall to supervise the entire structure. That year we had about a thousand undergraduates enrolled in the groups. At the same time Henry Wright had his freshman class in the life of Christ, with an average attendance of about one hundred. I attempted to know every man in the classes of 1909, 1910, and 1911, to be a kind of pastor to the leaders, and encouraged the latter to take the same attitude toward the members of their groups. For that purpose I prepared a card with a daily prayer to be used by each leader. Never before had Yale had as many undergraduates in such groups and after I left the program dwindled. That it could have grown to such dimensions was evidence that most undergraduates were sympathetic and came from backgrounds which made participation natural. At that time the Student YMCA throughout the country was promoting voluntary Bible study classes. Yale simply did more than some others. In later years I often wondered how much we at Yale really accomplished in an intelligent knowledge of the Scriptures and a growth in Christian character.

Possessed by the compulsive conviction which had driven me to prepare for foreign missions, I believed that every Christian student should show reason why he should not become a missionary. I therefore approached

many undergraduates with that appeal. My contacts
through Dwight Hall and the Bible study groups gave
many opportunities. Out of that college generation, especially in the classes of 1909, 1910, and 1911, came a
number of missionaries. How far, if at all, I was responsible for their decision I do not know, and it is not very
important. From the class of 1909, which I knew
throughout its four years, with possibly one exception,
came more missionaries than from any other class in the
history of Yale College. That exception was the class
of 1892. In actual years of service as missionaries 1909
surpassed all other classes except 1892.

A potent influence in 1909 was William Whiting Borden. He was from a wealthy Chicago family. His older
brother, John, was in my class. John's daughter became
the wife of Adlai Stevenson. Bill's father died in Bill's
sophomore year and Bill's share of the estate was several
hundred thousand dollars. Bill's mother was a member of
the Moody Church in Chicago and was thoroughly committed to its position. In his year between the Hill School
and Yale, his mother had sent Bill around the world with
a prospective missionary as a companion. While in England, on the way home, partly as a result of a Keswick
Conference, Bill made a full commitment to Christ. He
entered Yale purposing to be a missionary. He planned to
go to a real frontier, the Moslems in West China, and to
seek appointment under the China Inland Mission. He
was an able student, President of Phi Beta Kappa in his
senior year. He was athletic, of great energy, handsome,
and a born leader of men. He could have excelled in
business or in almost any profession. He was conservative theologically, a firm believer in prayer. Outstanding,
he had a profound influence on the members of his class
and I feel sure that his missionary vision was a major
factor in the record of 1909 in missions. After Yale he
entered Princeton Theological Seminary and graduated.
Then he went to Egypt to study Arabic, planning to go
from there to China for the Chinese language. While in

Cairo he was taken with spinal meningitis and died
(1912). His biography, *Borden of Yale, '09*, written
by Mrs. Howard Taylor at his mother's request, has had a
profound influence on successive generations of students.
I look back on his friendship as one of the richest that I
have known.

CHAPTER III

THE MISSIONARY YEARS

My missionary years may be said to have begun in the autumn of 1909. For the ensuing academic year I was a travelling secretary of the Student Volunteer Movement for Foreign Missions. The Movement then had the practice of sending through the colleges, universities, and divinity schools several recent graduates who were about to go as missionaries with the appeal to join in that calling. Since I was under appointment by the Yale Foreign Missionary Society and had been active in approaching students at Yale, I was deemed a "natural" for the post. A few younger missionaries, not far from student age, were also on the staff. It was the year of a "quadrennial convention," the purpose of which was to present to each student generation the claims and opportunities of the missionary enterprise, and great efforts were put forth to recruit the right kind of delegations. With that in mind I was sent to several of the colleges in New England, the Middle States, and Michigan. The "quadrennial" was held in Rochester, New York. As Chairman of the Executive Committee of the Movement, John R. Mott presided, and, as he always did, made a profound impression. I had come to know him at the Northfield Conferences, where he presided, and where I was an annual attendant. After the "quadrennial" I visited a number of colleges, chiefly in New England and the North Atlantic States, to follow up the impressions made, and was sent to universities in the Middle West, and to Stanford and the University of California in Berkeley. Everywhere I spoke to small groups, some of them in fraternity houses, and made a special point of friendship with individuals. The year began an avocation of "collecting" colleges and universities—of seeing as many as possible—a hobby that I have cultivated through the years. More important, it brought several friendships, a few of which were to be lifelong. As during my student years at Yale, I seemed to sense those individuals who actually or potentially shared my Christian faith and had unusual gifts of leadership and of influencing others. As I had with each of my successive leaders of groups at Yale and others there who impressed me, I remembered them regularly in prayer and kept in touch with them by correspondence. Several decided to become missionaries. But I was aware that at most I was a catalyst, coming at a time when life purposes were being formed by young men whose home and church background predisposed them to consider missions. I also came to know a number of men who were already "student volunteers" and I endeavored to strengthen their purpose. Among the men whom I met that year several were later outstanding missionaries.

At the Yale Commencement in 1910, at the annual meeting of Yale-in-China, I was commissioned. The speaker was Yung Wing of the class of 1853, the first Chinese to graduate from an American college, and distinguished as the initiator and director of the Chinese Educational Mission, which brought approximately a hundred Chinese lads to study in the United States. Ruddy of face, with iron-grey hair and flashing eyes, he made a great impression on me. I remember gratefully that after the others had gone, Dean and Mrs. Wright lingered to give me an affectionate farewell.

At the end of the Northfield Conference of 1910 I went to China by way of Europe. Since most of my family were on the West Coast, the only relative to see me off was a cousin of my mother who lived in Brooklyn and had been a warm friend during my Yale years. Characteristically,

Henry Wright made a special trip from his summer re-
treat in Oakham to bid me *bon voyage*. In our evening
devotions he gave me a verse which he suggested that I
take as a guide: "I can do all things through Christ, who
strengthens me." I have not fully lived up to it, but it has
been with me through the years.

On that first of many trips to Europe, I had only about
three weeks in England and on the Continent, for I could
not leave the States until after Northfield, about July 5th.
The Yale-in-China trustees charged me to reach China in
time to arrive in Kuling, the major summer resort in the
mid-Yangtze Valley, before the missionaries had scat-
tered for their autumn work, and thus meet that gallant
company. I landed at Plymouth, and packed full a wonderful ten days in the radiant English summer. I had a
day in the Lake District, attended a conference of the British Student Christian Movement at Baslow in the Peak
District of Derbyshire, and saw briefly Haddon Hall,
Coventry, Kenilworth, Warwick, Oxford, Cambridge, Ely,
London, and Canterbury. In Oxford and Cambridge I
looked in at each of the colleges. Halfway between the
two towns I spent a night at Bedford, made famous by
Bunyan. I had about two days in Paris, took a night train
to Geneva and spent a day at Interlaken, where my win-
dow looked out on the Jungfrau under a full moon. I did
not have time to scale the mountain, but I took a train to
the foot. Then came a Sunday in Lucerne with a climb of
the Rigi in the afternoon. A brief glimpse of Munich was
followed by a night at Garmisch-Partenkirchen in the
Bavarian Alps, and the Passion Play at Oberammergau.
From there I went to Berlin, but with a brief stop between trains at Nuremberg, a night in Heidelberg, the
steamer trip down the Rhine from Mainz to Bonn, and a
glimpse of Halle, chosen because of its association with
the early Pietist missions. In Berlin, Bill Borden and I had
a weekend together. I then took a train to Moscow to catch
the Trans-Siberian express. On the train I met a young
Englishman of about my age who was travelling for the

Sunlight Soap Company of Liverpool. He had letters to
British merchants in Moscow. They took us to the Krem-
lin, where for the first time I heard a Russian choir, gave
us dinner, and put us on our train. The Wagon-Lits Company ran a weekly express for Western Europeans and
Americans, with excellent sleeping cars and diner. On
the train were some Americans who knew missionary
friends of mine. Fred Fisher, a cousin, was Consul-
General at Mukden. He had alerted the consul at Harbin,
Roger Greene, whom I later knew as the Director of the
Peking Union Medical College. He and his sister were at
the station to see me on my way. Fred Fisher had me for
dinner and put me on the night train for Peking in
charge of his consular assistant, Nelson Johnson, who
years later was American Ambassador to China. Through
Nelson Johnson I was entertained in Peking by the young
men who were studying Chinese in preparation for the
consular service. With him and one of the students,
Esson Gale, I began lifelong friendships. At Hankow,
which was my next stop, I was met by an Episcopal
missionary who was bound for Kuling and who courteously escorted me to that mountain valley. All the six
weeks from the States had been marked by many kind-
nesses, some from entire strangers, some from American
student acquaintances arising in my year with the Student Volunteer Movement, and others from missionaries.
At Kuling I was introduced to the missionaries of many
denominations assembled there for the summer and had
a little glimpse of the missionary fellowship which across
the years has been one of the richest experiences of life.
In connection with it I often think of the line from the *Te
Deum*: "The glorious company of the Apostles praise
Thee." As I was to learn, missionaries are not without
their faults and compass a great variety in character,
ability, and idiosyncrasies, but they have a tie in a common dedication and a common loyalty and can always be
counted on for hospitality and entirely undeserved kindness.

Standing out vividly in my memory of those first days in Kuling was a brief conversation with Timothy Richard, the Welsh Baptist, then in late middle life. Erect, with ivory hair, ruddy face, and flashing eyes, he would attract attention in any company. He had worked and dreamed in terms of all China—in personal evangelism, in fighting famine, and in seeking to aid the Chinese leaders as they sought to adjust to the invasion of the Occident. He thought and planned in terms of the conversion of all the Chinese. When I was introduced to him he asked my plans. Embarrassed, I stammered something about what Yale-in-China was attempting. I have never forgotten his kindly but challenging impatience. "In how large terms are you planning?" he cried.

A few days before the autumn term of the school began I went to Changsha, where the Yale Mission was situated. I was met by William J. Hail, the one member of the foreign staff then in the city. He took me to the School. Classes had been begun four years before, in 1906. The School had purchased property near the center of the city. It contained a courtyard, dormitories for the students, a dining hall, classrooms, a chapel, quarters for the unmarried foreign staff and for one of the families. It was a Middle School, preparatory to the college for which our plans called. Across the street were a small hospital and clinic. The American staff was Edward H. Hume (Yale 1897 and Johns Hopkins 1901) and his family, Brownell Gage (1898) and his family, his sister Nina Gage, a nurse, William Hail, Dickson Leavens, and I. Brownell and Nina Gage were on furlough, and Bill Hail (1906D), Dick Leavens (1909), and I were the "Bachelors' Mess," for which we had three servants, chief among them a cook trained in Western cuisine by a missionary wife. Hume was the physician and surgeon. He had a remarkable command of Chinese, spoken and written, and had already begun to make contacts with prominent Chinese that were to facilitate the development of a medical school. A Yale-trained Chinese physi-

cian, F. C. Yen, was on the staff on equal status with the
Americans, for from the beginning the ideal, then rela-
tively novel, was to have the Mission a joint Chinese-
American enterprise.

Changsha was the capital of Hunan Province, and had
not been opened to foreign residence until after the sup-
pression of the anti-foreign Boxer Outbreak of 1900-
1901. It was an ancient city, begun several centuries
before the time of Christ. Graves, of which we
were then unaware but which some years later were
uncovered by the driving through of roads and Communist archeology, contained remains of early wealthy in-
habitants. Above ground when I arrived was a city of
about 200,000, housed in one- and two-story dwellings,
with Confucian and Buddhist shrines, crisscrossed by
narrow streets, and encompassed by a wall about five
miles in circumference. The wall averaged about forty
feet in height and at the top was about twelve feet wide.
Changsha was part of the ancient high culture which
had been standard for all East Asia and a city in an
empire which was more than two thousand years old and
had been the mightiest on the eastern side of the Eurasi-
atic Continent. We were vividly aware of the fact that
that culture was in the early throes of a major revolution
which was transforming every aspect of life. The revolution was without precedent in the long history of the
empire. It was being wrought by the impact of Western
peoples. The impact had begun to produce a crack in the
encircling wall about seventy years before—through the
First Anglo-Chinese War (1839-1842). The crack had
been slightly widened a little over sixty years earlier by a
second war in which the French had joined the English
(1856-1860). It had become a rift fifteen years and then
five years earlier through the defeat of China by Japan
(1894-1895) and the Russo-Japanese War (1904-1905),
the latter fought mostly on Chinese soil. Late in the
1890's the partition of China among earth-hungry Euro-

peans seemed imminent and the land was divided into "spheres of influence." Changsha was in the British sphere, a sphere which embraced the entire Yangtze Valley. The customs were collected by the Imperial Maritime Customs Service, whose head and most of whose ranking members, while technically Chinese officials, were British. British gunboats and British passenger steamers plied the waters of the Yangtze and its tributaries. Following the Boxer Outbreak (1900-1901) China was in reality an occupied country. The rift was widening into a collapse. Five years earlier (1905) the civil service examinations, a major bulwark of Confucianism, the traditional ideological basis of Chinese culture, had been abolished. As a symbol the stalls in which the examinations had been held in Changsha were removed and an unsightly, flimsy structure in pseudo-Western style had been erected on one corner of the site as headquarters of the provincial "educational association." In 1911-1912, during my second year in China, the Confucian monarchy was swept into the discard and in its place was what was hopefully called "the Republic of China," begun by the leaders of a people who, although undoubtedly able, were completely inexperienced in a political structure which that name was meant to designate.

We of the Yale Mission were part of the invading culture. We sometimes felt as though we were Martians who had invaded the earth, so contrasting were the cultures and so catastrophic the results. But we were aware that the changes would have come had we never arrived. We were hoping that in our small way we could help to modify them wholesomely by contributing to the formation of youth who, learning the best of the old and the new and inspired by the Christian faith, would aid in the emergence of a China all the better from the inevitable and painful transition. Through our hospital, soon to grow into a medical school and a school of nursing, by the skills developed in the Occident, we could contribute

toward the alleviation of suffering. Significantly, Mao
Tse-tung and Liu Shao-ch'i, both natives of Hunan, became students in Changsha, but not in the Yale School.
Had they come to us their future and that of China might
have been different from that of the 1950's and 1960's.

Several other Protestant missions were in Changsha,
nearly all less than ten years on the scene. They included
American Episcopalians, American Evangelicals (Homer
Dubs, the son of its head and then in his teens, was later
to be Professor of Chinese in Oxford), Norwegian Luth-
erans, English Wesleyans, the Christian and Missionary
Alliance, and a German affiliate of the China Inland Mission. In addition there was an independent "faith" missionary from the United States. The next year was to see
the arrival of Seventh-Day Adventists. Some of the missions encouraged their boys to come to our school.

During the first year my major assignment was the
study of Chinese. For that, textbooks prepared by missionaries were available and I had the full time of an
intelligent Chinese scholar who had had experience in
teaching some of my predecessors in the Yale Mission. I
also taught a class in American history, played the organ
in chapel, had a Bible class in English for two sons of a
Chinese official and not in the School, organized a glee
club, and had an informal group of the boys in the
School. In addition I organized and was the secretary of a
group of Chinese and missionaries who were interested in
becoming acquainted. Among the Chinese were some
men of prominence, one of them a holder of the highest
degree in the civil service examinations, son of a former
governor, and later to be several times governor of
Hunan. I remember him gratefully for his delicate unos-
tentatious courtesy to a young foreigner who was beginning to stammer a little Chinese. The members of the
group gave one another dinners and from time to time
one of the Chinese addressed students of the city
gathered in our chapel.

For exercise we "bachelors" climbed a high hill across the river, took long walks in the country, and in wet weather between tea and dinner made the circuit of the top of the city wall. During the long winter vacation we hiked across the province about a hundred miles to visit a fellow Yale man who had a mission school for boys. We had coolies carry our food and our bedding and slept in Chinese inns.

At the end of the school year most of the Yale Mission staff went to Kuling for the summer. There I continued the study of Chinese and engaged in long hikes. Toward the end of the summer I had an attack of amoebic dysentery which proved my undoing. That was a new experience, for I had never before been in bed from illness for as much as a day. The treatment was drastic, the amoebae seemed to be destroyed, but what proved to be permanent damage was done to the colon. Strength did not return and when my colleagues left to begin the fall term I remained on. After a short time I was kindly given care in a sanatorium run by a British physician and surgeon of the China Inland Mission who had had to remain on the mountain for his own health. After some weeks he removed my appendix, which surgery proved to have been a source of minor attacks, undiagnosed, since my boyhood. For various reasons a few other missionaries were in Kuling for the winter, so I was not without company. On October 10, 1911, three days before I had surgery, the revolution which upset the dynasty broke out in Wuchang, farther up the Yangtze. Shortly after Christmas I returned to Changsha and resumed the study of Chinese. But strength did not fully return. In March I left for the United States, hoping that a long summer in my old home in Oregon would bring complete restoration. So confident was I of resuming my work in Changsha that I purchased a round-trip ticket on a Yangtze steamer.

The revolution was in full swing. On my way to Shanghai I paused in Nanking, then the provisional capital of the Republic. A Yale friend, C. T. Wang, was in the newly elected Senate. As I went to see him I had to make my way through a crowd of Chinese women who were demanding voting privileges for their sex. They were evidence of the drastic changes which were beginning.

CHAPTER IV

CONVALESCENCE

With brief stops in Nagasaki, Yokohama, with time enough to see Kamakura and Tokyo, and Honolulu, a slow Pacific steamer brought me to San Francisco. A Southern Pacific train promptly carried me to Oregon City. But the hoped-for quick recovery did not come. Evidently I had been forcing my body beyond its strength. With the opportunity for relaxation in the familiar home atmosphere the bottom dropped out. Any physical exertion was difficult and any mental activity impossible. I could not do even light reading for more than a few minutes at a time. Deep mental depression followed— fortunately with no thought of suicide. The family was extremely kind and the family physician very patient and wise. No clear diagnosis was achieved. I was said to be suffering from "nervous prostration." Clearly, return to China in the autumn was out of the question. I tried every suggestion that seemed promising. Microscopic examination failed to show surviving amoebae. The rector of the leading Episcopal Church in Portland was having success in employing prayer in healing. I went to him and, without words, he put his hands on my head, praying silently with intense concentration, but little or no improvement followed. When ability to read revived, as it did gradually, I went through *Science and Health with Key to the Scriptures* and other suggested books on the use of individual prayer. Physical strength returned first. To use my hands, I began caring for the family's yard.

Fortunately the home stood in ample grounds: I mowed the lawn and tended the trees and shrubs. In January I went for a month to the state agricultural college in Corvallis and took short courses in vegetable gardening and pruning and grafting fruit trees. In Oregon City I applied them in the familiar grounds, in planting and caring for a large vegetable garden, and in setting out roses and nut trees. The yard still gives evidence of the labors of those days. One form of recreation which I continue to enjoy is pruning fruit trees and shrubs—in summers in the old home and on Saturday afternoons during the academic year with Fulton Ferguson on his country place, for he enjoys the same activities.

By the summer and autumn of 1913 I was sufficiently restored to do a few hours of mental work each day. I employed them in reading Chinese—chiefly the *Four Books*—and memorizing large sections of the *Analects*. I either sent for or had brought with me the necessary texts, translations, and dictionaries. I also helped in the editing of the *Letters of Ezra Fisher*, written to the American Baptist Home Mission Society. They were later privately printed and some appeared in the *Quarterly* of the Oregon Historical Society.

By the summer of 1914 I was enough improved to undertake part-time regular teaching, but was not yet ready for China. I decided to apply to Reed College, for of the Oregon colleges it was physically the nearest to my home. If appointed, I could easily come home weekends or whenever that seemed desirable. Reed College had recently been founded and its first classes had been held. I had not met the President, and without an introduction early in July I made an appointment. I told him my story and my hope of regaining enough strength to return to China. He was very kind but said that the budget had been made out and students had already elected their program for the ensuing year. But he asked me to come back in a few weeks. When I returned, in August, war had broken out in Europe. The President said that in light of that fact I could teach one course a semester— the first on the recent history of Europe and the second on the Far East. I could give an extension course in the Portland Public Library on the European background of the war and could advise the Christian Association. I could have a room in the men's dormitory, eat in the dining hall, and go home over the weekends or whenever I needed that escape.

Then began two very interesting and stimulating years. The President, William Trufant Foster, was young, about thirty years of age. A graduate of Harvard, where he had worked his way through, and with a Ph. D. from Columbia, his previous teaching had most recently been at Bowdoin. The trustees of Reed College had given him a year after his appointment to work out his plans and to select his faculty. He had great dreams of building a unique college, trying new and progressive methods. With that as a lure he had attracted an extraordinary faculty, young (the oldest was forty and some were still in their twenties), most of them with Ph. D.'s from Eastern universities, and all eager to share in the adventure. The college had what for those days was a large endowment, for practically the entire estate of Simeon and Amanda Reed, a childless couple, had been left for the founding. Foster was able to offer good salaries, erect an excellent plant on a large campus, and begin an adequate equipment of libraries and laboratories. I soon learned that his kindness to me was typical. During my two years at Reed he rescued other young scholars from difficult academic situations. Yet he assured himself that they had high potential. The year after I left the later Senator Douglas of Illinois was for a year on the faculty. During my first year physics was taught by Karl Compton, eventually President of the Massachusetts Institute of Technology. An instructor in political science, Robert D. Leigh, who came in my second year, became the first President of Bennington College. During my two years the chair of economics and sociology was held by William G. Ogburn, whose main career was as an honor professor of sociology at the University of Chicago. The President's secretary, Florence M. Read, was for many years the creative head of Spellman College, part of Atlanta University and the best college for Negro girls. For a time she was acting President of Atlanta University. Both students and faculty were stimulated by the atmosphere. One member of the faculty described us aptly as "Comrades of the Quest." Intellectually Reed College was the most stimulating environment that I had thus far known. Religiously, Reed had no denominational connections, but the Chairman of the Trustees, at whose suggestion the bequest which founded the college had been made, was Thomas Lamb Eliot, son of the Eliot who had founded Washington University in St. Louis. He was the first pastor of the Unitarian Church in Portland, a saintly man of great charm and high culture, who was one of the most eminent and public-spirited citizens of the city. No courses in religion were offered, but a daily chapel was held at which attendance was voluntary, at which the majority of students were regularly present, and which all members of the faculty took turns in leading.

During both my years at Reed I continued physical recuperation, partly by caring for the grounds of my Oregon City home and partly by engaging vigorously in tennis, handball, and boxing. Previously I had not participated in such sports, but I went into them deliberately. While never especially proficient in them, I enjoyed them.

In both years I had Harry Moore as a roommate. Harry was about my age, had been delayed in his education, and at the time was in charge of the Oregon Social Hygiene Society. In later years he initiated a special program for the alcohol problem. In middle life he died of cancer.

Since returning from China I had been deeply impressed by the lack of information about the Far East in this country. So far as I knew, in only seven colleges and universities were any courses being offered on China or Japan and, so far as I could discover, nothing was being done in any high school. I believed myself called to be a trail blazer. During my second year at Reed I began writing articles in educational and historical journals calling attention to the vacuum. To help fill it I wrote a little book, *The Development of China*, to serve as a textbook in introductory courses. It was accepted by Houghton Mifflin. Because it met a need, it went into several revised editions and was in print for more than thirty years. In June, 1915, I shared in Reed's first commencement.

During my second year at Reed I taught two courses, which was half the normal load. I began wondering whether it would be wise ever to return to China.

Officially I was still on leave from Changsha. Indeed, I did not formally resign until 1917. But since March, 1912, I had not asked or received financial aid from the Yale Foreign Missionary Society.

Toward the end of the second year Reed's administration had to tell me that the budget would not permit keeping me on full time, for when I arrived history had a full-time man who of course would remain and my appointment was annual and as an emergency. I had to face the decision of my future. I considered going professionally into a resident secretaryship of the Student YMCA. After my experience in Dwight Hall that would have been natural. Indeed, an offer came of such a post in one of the better Eastern universities. However, as I had observed that occupation I became convinced that it did not offer a lifetime of service. As the age-gap widened, close and helpful contacts with students—my chief interest—would become more difficult. But college teaching presented no such obstacle. I therefore decided on the latter. Efforts to find an opening in a college faculty appeared blocked. However, in June, through the kindness of an old friend of McMinnville days, Leonard W.

Riley, by that time President of the college, an invitation came from President Chamberlain of Denison University to a one-year appointment in history and the hint was given, indirectly, that if I proved satisfactory permanency was assured.

I continue to be profoundly thankful for the Reed years. But in retrospect I am convinced that had I remained I could not have made my largest contribution. Some years later Foster's successor asked me to return, but I promptly declined. Religiously the atmosphere would increasingly have been uncongenial and I could not have altered it. Moreover, not many of my Reed colleagues remained for more than a few years. From time to time faculty dissensions marred the morale. Reed has continued, deservedly, to have an outstanding reputation in the academic world and some of the alumni have achieved distinction in the professions, but a kind of self-conscious intellectual pride, especially in the departments of the humanities, would to me have proved basically stultifying. However, I can never be sufficiently grateful to William Foster for giving me the Reed opportunity. He did not remain at Reed for many years. But until his death we were warm friends and I was glad to dedicate to him a textbook, *A Short History of the Far East,* in memory of his kindness. With some others of my Reed contemporaries—faculty and students—lifelong friendships were formed.

CHAPTER V

THE DENISON YEARS

The appointment to Denison proved to be an introduction to one of the richest experiences of life. I found myself in a college in which I quickly felt at home. The physical setting was charming. Granville had been settled by New Englanders and the village seemed as though it had been transplanted from the Connecticut Valley. At the four corners at the middle of its main street were churches. The main street, appropriately named Broadway, was bordered by huge shade trees, and down its center ran a narrow, grassy lawn. Most of the college buildings were on a hill, a hundred feet or so above the village. In many ways Denison reminded me of McMinnville College, except that it had a larger faculty and student body and was better equipped physically. Its students were mostly from Baptist families. Social life was simple and wholesome. Fraternities and sororities existed, but their houses were modest. Little formal instruction in Bible or religion was given, but daily chapel was required and the YMCA and YWCA were strong and the former had part of a building assigned to it. Arthur Brumback, my favorite teacher at McMinnville, was an alumnus and had been head of the chemistry department. He had died the preceding summer, but his widow continued to live in Granville and I rented a room in her home. The students numbered about seven hundred fifty, of whom a few were in Doane Academy, the preparatory department discontinued a little later because of the

growth of high schools. About three-fifths of the student
body were men and two-fifths women.

The first year I taught all the history and, inevitably,
included a course on the Far East. An assistant professor
of history was on leave to complete his work for the
doctorate and after being awarded the degree did not
return. Before the Christmas recess the President offered
me a full professorship on tenure.

Part of the first Christmas vacation I spent in New
Haven, en route to a student conference at Northfield.
There Harlan Page Beach called me aside and made a
suggestion which was later to bring me back to Yale. He
was Yale's first professor of missions, holder of the D.
Willis James chair in that subject. He had about four
years before he reached the age when emeritus status
would be compulsory. He said that he had no authority to
make me an offer, but that he would like me to succeed
him. He asked me to promise not to accept an offer to
leave Denison without first giving him an opportunity to
see whether a formal call could be given me. I did as he
asked, but did not promise to accept if the call came. On
returning to Denison I told President Chamberlain of the
conversation and asked whether to test myself out in the
field I might offer a course in missions. He kindly agreed,
and the following year I scheduled a semester course in
the history of the expansion of Christianity and gave it
each of the succeeding years. Out of it eventually grew
my major course at Yale and the seven volumes which in
dimensions are my *magnum opus*. Eugene Exman was
then an undergraduate at Denison and took the course.

My second year I was made head of the Department of
History and Political Science, for the chairman resigned
to become President of Franklin College. The department
included history, economics, sociology, and political
science, but I did not teach anything but history. Never
during my Denison years did the department staff have
more than five members. Denison's traditional strength
had been in the natural sciences.

During my first year at Denison the United States entered the First World War. Military drill was immediately introduced. When conscription came, as it did in most American colleges and universities, the campus was transformed into a military camp and the men were enrolled in the Student Army Training Corps.

I had to face the problem of my part in the war. Because I was now known as a specialist on the Far East, a tentative offer came for a position in the Far Eastern section of the Department of State with an army commission. Because I believed that I could best serve by helping maintain the ordinary processes of civilization through remaining in the college, I declined. But, being unmarried, if I was not to be caught in the draft, ordination seemed advisable. Because of my interests it was a natural step and the emergency only hastened it. In the summer of 1918 I was ordained in the Baptist Church in Oregon City. Most of the ordaining council had known me since childhood. To me the service was a benediction, as though the members were expressing their trust and in the laying on of hands were placing me in the apostolic succession. On returning to Granville I was appointed chaplain of Denison, adding that responsibility to my other duties. I was the first to have that post.

With most of my contemporaries I had never been confronted with the issue of pacifism, for war had seemed impossible. While deploring the war and in my class in modern European history pointing out that international friendships and enmities were notoriously unstable, the allies of today being the enemies of tomorrow and the deadly enemies of today later becoming sworn friends, I honestly believed that under existing circumstances American participation in the war was the lesser of two evils. However, a few of the men of my age whom I knew in student Christian circles took the pacifist stand and served heroically in relief activities in highly dangerous situations. Their conviction and sacrificial consistency troubled me. My only active participation in the war

effort was to serve for part of a summer with the YMCA
at Camp Devens in Massachusetts where Henry Wright
and others of my Yale friends were on the staff. Growing
out of World War I and the dream of making the world
"safe for democracy" was a little book of Bible studies,
The Christian Basis of World Democracy, which I wrote
soon after the coming of peace.

During my Denison years I persisted in blazing trails in
Far Eastern studies. In 1916-1917 I wrote *The Development of Japan* as a companion to *The Development of
China.* It went through several revised editions, eventually, at the request of the publishers, the Macmillan Company, as *The History of Japan.* It was in print for about
fifty years and in 1963 the Indian government purchased
the right of translating it. I began attending the annual
meetings of the American Historical Association and at
my instance the Far East was given a place on successive
programs.

During my Denison years I began collecting material
for what developed into my first large book, *A History of
Christian Missions in China.* Here, too, I was blazing new
trails. No one had ever comprehensively and thoroughly
covered the subject. I included in it all branches of the
Church—Protestant, Roman Catholic, and Russian Orthodox. That also was new—what might be described as
an ecumenical undertaking, an attempt without espous-
ing any one church to tell the entire story. I placed the
story in the setting of the total impact of the West on
China. During 1919 and 1920 I put in part of the summer in New Haven, taking notes in the Day Missions
Library. As a companion I had David E. Owen, a history
major. We spent the working day in the library, and in
the late afternoon played tennis.

Incidental to this project, in the summer of 1919 we
formed a close association with an interesting group,
most of them undergraduates who were enrolled in the
summer term of the Law School. One of the number, son
of a China missionary of the Yale class of 1892, to pay

expenses was managing a small dining group in the Alpha Delta Phi house. He asked Dave Owen and me to join them. That was Henry W. Luce. In the group were Britton Hadden, who with Luce was soon to found *Time*, Charles Taft, younger son of the President, Robert M. Hutchins, later to be President and then Chancellor of the University of Chicago and creator of the Fund of the Republic, George Van Sanford, an instructor in English, eventually headmaster of Hotchkiss and a member of the Yale Corporation, and Alfred Bellinger, an instructor in the classics, later to be acting Dean of Yale College.

I continued to be active in the Student Volunteer Movement and the Student YMCA. Since the war prevented the regular quadrennial, in the Christmas recess of 1916-1917 a smaller one was held at Northfield. I attended and met old friends and made new ones. After the war I was on the editorial board of *The Intercollegian*, the periodical of the Student YMCA. In connection with it I met Henry Pitney Van Dusen, then a student in Union Theological Seminary and on the staff of the Madison Avenue Presbyterian Church. David R. Porter, a former Rhodes scholar, as head of the Student YMCA was the editor and at his request I wrote articles and editorials for the magazine. It was at the instance of David Porter that in the Christmas recess of 1920-1921 I represented the Student Department of the YMCA at the quadrennial of the British Student Christian Movement in Glasgow. There for the first time I heard William Temple and met others who were to become fast friends. In the journey from Glasgow to my steamer I had glimpses of Edinburgh, Durham, York, and Lincoln.

Because of the deep interest in individuals which was a major reason for going into teaching, my energies at Denison were chiefly directed toward students. Early I was made chairman of the faculty's Student Affairs Committee. Its functions were advisory, not disciplinary. I

soon learned the occasions in the academic year which
might precipitate student explosions and ahead of time
would suggest to the president of the student council
that he quietly take steps to forestall them. As a result
during my tenure of the office few of them developed.
Soon after the war several of the students organized the
Denison Commons Club. The fraternities provided social
facilities for the majority of the men. However, a substantial minority were not in them. The literary societies
which once were an alternative were moribund. President Chamberlain was concerned, learned of Commons
Clubs in several of the Eastern colleges, and brought them
to the attention of some non-fraternity men. He wisely
did it in such fashion that a few of the abler of their
number seized upon the idea as though it was their own.
They effected an organization, centering it about "Aunt
Ida" who had had a number of them as boarders. They
obtained use of a house and before long the President
assigned them a dormitory which they could control for
rooming, dining, and social purposes. Their officers asked
me to join them. Since Denison had no chapter of Alpha
Chi Rho and I could accept without violating my obligations to that organization, I gladly assented. I urged on
the founders the adoption of the "open door" as a basic
principle—namely, asking into membership every un-
affiliated man and allowing any who wished to with-
draw, whether to join a fraternity or for any other reason. The project enlisted some of the ablest students,
among them several who later became distinguished in
scholarship, teaching, the ministry, and business. They
stimulated the formation of Commons Clubs in several
Midwestern colleges and universities, organized a national association, and asked me to become the latter's
first President. This I did toward the end of my last year
at Denison, and served for one term.

In several ways I formed friendships with undergraduates. During springs and autumns I played tennis with

them. I dined at their fraternities and hiked with them. I had them as secretaries to do my letters. Chief among the latter was Robert Abernathy, charming, able, who several years later went to Oxford, married, and died soon after he had begun teaching at the Hill School. To numbers of the men I presented foreign missions as a challenge. A few responded and gave outstanding service. Some I counselled in scholarship and aided in their initial attempts at writing. I came to know most of the students. Obviously, as a bachelor, I could not form intimate friendships with any of the girls, but some I knew well.

Out of the Denison years grew many lasting friendships, some with colleagues and some with students, and I have rejoiced to keep them warm. From the student body of 1916-1921 came several who were to be eminent in the professions. Some were clergymen, notably Harold Cook Phillips, long outstanding as a preacher and pastor in Cleveland; Theodore F. Adams, eventually President of the Baptist World Alliance and one of the outstanding citizens of Richmond, Virginia, as pastor of its First Baptist Church; and his brother Earl, pastor and then administrator. Others were scholars and administrators. After useful years as a missionary in the Congo, Dana Albaugh gave valiant service as a secretary of the American Baptist Foreign Mission Society. George Cressey was on the faculty of Shanghai Baptist University, became the world's major geographer of China, and ended his career as chairman of the Department of Geography of Syracuse University. His brother, Paul, after briefly teaching in China, for years was on the faculty of Wheaton College in Norton, Massachusetts, and in his emeritus years taught in the Philippines. William Rhodes became head of the American Baptist Home Mission Society. Howard Jefferson, after a Yale Ph. D. and teaching at Colgate, was for years President of Clark University. David Owen developed into one of the most popular teachers of history

in Harvard, for a time headed Harvard's History Department, and for years was the greatly loved head of one of
the Harvard houses. Donald Atwell was a YMCA secretary in Egypt and in a Pittsburgh suburb. After some
years as a missionary in Peru, Bert Hodges was long on
the administrative staff of Denison. As the creative head
of the religion department of Harper & Brothers (later
Harper & Row) Eugene Exman was eventually the country's outstanding publisher of books on religion. Still others were noted in business and as laymen in churches.

In the spring of 1920, after the war, colleges and
universities were replenishing their faculties. Since I was
young and had done some publishing, several "feelers"
and outright invitations came. One was to be president of
a well-established college. I quickly discouraged it, for I
felt that my services should not be in administration. I
learned that an offer was probably on the way from the
University of Wisconsin for Far Eastern studies, where
Reinsch, who had resigned to become Minister to China,
had taught in the field. From the University of
Chicago was an urgent offer to be the first holder of a
chair of missions. An approach from Northwestern was
made to be an associate in missions and comparative
religion to Edmund Soper, soon to become a warm friend.
As in duty bound I let Harlan Beach know of the offers
and before many weeks an invitation came to succeed
him on his retirement, due in 1921. Characteristically
and generously he offered to retire a year early if that
would bring my acceptance. I was deeply troubled. I had
no desire to leave Denison. Indeed I would have pre-
ferred remaining there for life, and President Chamberlain, whom I told of the offers as they came, kindly urged
me to stay. Here was the old question which had made
me a missionary: What was God's will? Where could I
best serve His purposes? I consulted many friends in
New York and Chicago. I wrote William Foster of my
problem. He asked me not to make a decision until we

could talk it over, for he was coming East and could stop off in Granville. I agreed. He spoke at chapel for me. Then, as we lay in twin beds in my sleeping porch, I placed before him several possibilities. By that time I had about decided to go to Yale. He agreed, and the next day I sent my acceptance.

My reasons for the Yale post were several. I could resume my connections with Dwight Hall and Yale undergraduates. More important, I could fulfill my missionary purpose by helping to prepare missionaries, by presenting missions as a life work to undergraduates and to students in the Divinity School, by acquainting future pastors with foreign missions, by serving on boards and committees in New York which had to do with the world mission, and by writing. The Day Missions Library, begun and endowed by Professor and Mrs. George Day and organized and greatly augmented by Professor Beach, offered unexcelled facilities for research in missions. In addition, I could continue my contribution to Far Eastern studies by offering one course a year in some aspect of the vast subject. As was true in signing the Student Volunteer declaration in 1904, I went to the Yale faculty from a sheer sense of duty. I am now certain, as I am about the Student Volunteer declaration, that I was seeing dimly, but decisively, the divine purpose for my life. But many years were to pass before this became clear. As will appear in a later chapter, my first decade at Yale, as were my months in China, was troubled and frustrating. But from the perspective of old age I am certain that what looked like sacrifice was the door to the fullest use of the capacities with which God had endowed me and, in these later days, to an unbelievably rich and quietly happy life.

Again and again I have been back to Granville, often as a lecturer, and increasingly I am grateful for the connection and also for the decision to leave the faculty. The academic quality of the institution has greatly improved, but the character of the student body has been basically altered. I could not have made the contributions through it that I did in the five years that I was on the staff. The opportunities which in 1920 I dimly saw at Yale have more than amply opened and even in my emeritus years have enlarged.

CHAPTER VI

THE FIRST DECADE ON THE YALE FACULTY

As I have suggested, the first ten years on the Yale faculty were very difficult. That was not because the doors which had led me to decide to accept the Yale offer were non-existent or closed. All the doors were even more widely open than I had anticipated. Rather it was because of the problems presented by the doors. Coming as I did to the D. Willis James Professorship of Missions as successor to Harlan Page Beach, widely recognized as the most eminent contemporary academic specialist on missions in the United States, much was expected of me in circles which had to do with the world mission. But to many on the Yale faculty and elsewhere in academic circles, missions seemed associated with propaganda and valid scholarship in the field was deemed unlikely. Moreover, the fact that I had specialized in East Asia proved an obstacle to early acceptance. Existing departments such as history and political science which normally would deal with the subject confined their attention to the Western world, and at best the Far East was very much on the fringe of their interest. Even in the Divinity School, to which the Yale Corporation rightly assigned me, missions was a late arrival and in view of the established disciplines, such as Bible, theology, and church history, was accorded a minor place on the curriculum.

On my arrival, the Divinity School was in the early stages of a fresh epoch in its history. I had scarcely known it in my student days. It then had only a small enrollment. Although technically undenominational, it was Congregational by long tradition and both its students and faculty had been chiefly of that denomination. The colleges which had once been its constituency were less a source of candidates for the ministry than formerly and around the turn of the century the applications for admission dwindled. A few years before I came on the faculty, Charles R. Brown was appointed Dean. He was eminent as a preacher, especially to colleges. Through him the student body steadily mounted and became larger and more varied denominationally than at any time in the previous history of the School. The faculty was distinguished and growing. Aside from Dean Brown, at the time its most widely known members, both with honorary degrees from European as well as American universities, were Benjamin W. Bacon, in New Testament, and Williston Walker, in church history. Walker was also Provost of the University. Some of the younger men were later to be fully as distinguished. Less than ten years earlier, Henry Wright had been appointed to the faculty in a professorship especially endowed for him, and began a program for preparing men for the lay ministry, especially in the city and Student YMCAs. Luther A. Weigle had recently come in religious education, and was already making the chair, named for Horace Bushnell, the outstanding one in the world, preparing men and women in what was then a young and growing discipline. Roland H. Bainton had begun teaching in 1920. After taking his doctorate in New Testament, he had been offered the choice of following Bacon or Walker, then not far from the emeritus status. He had chosen church history and was already outstanding as a teacher. The Divinity School was preparing to celebrate its centennial, due in 1922.

Almost immediately after my arrival, in September, 1921, doors began to open. In addition to my office in the building of the Day Missions Library, I chose to take rooms in the Divinity School, and had a suite of three, a study and two bedrooms, on the inner court. The study, with its fireplace, quickly became the meeting place of a weekly informal group of students on the floor. I had as roommate Dorence Cowles, a Denison friend, newly enrolled in the Medical School. I was elected to the trustees of Yale-in-China and early became chairman of its personnel committee, a post I was to occupy for about forty years. Contacts were quickly renewed with Dwight Hall. Its General Secretary, E. Fay Campbell, was completing his course in the Divinity School. He elected a course with me. He was headed for foreign missions, had been a travelling secretary of the Student Volunteer Movement, and it was only his wife's physical frailty which kept them from fulfilling that purpose. He had about two decades of notable service at Yale, making a major contribution to the religious life of the University. Our friendship continued through the years and with his children. I was elected to the Oriental Club, organized a few years before and embracing in its membership those interested in all aspects of that area, interpreted as stretching from the Hellespont to the Pacific Ocean. The tradition was for monthly meetings in the homes of the members. The membership, then small because of the relatively few on the faculty whose interests were in that region, eventually expanded. In my later years I was the oldest member and the one with the longest membership.

In the autumn of 1921 an invitation came from John R. Mott to become a member of the Committee of the World's Student Christian Federation and to attend its enlarged meeting in Peking in the spring of 1922. The University generously gave me permission on the condition that I would make arrangements for my work. Even more generously, Professor Beach agreed to take enough of my course load to meet that condition. I crossed on a steamer with some of the delegates, including Dr. and Mrs. Mott. In the party was an undergraduate from Northwestern University, Carl Rogers, obviously wholesome and able, but as yet giving no indications of his eventual distinctive contribution through his form of non-directive counselling.

Arriving in China, we found in progress an anti-religious, chiefly anti-Christian movement led by some of the intelligentsia, notably in the National University in Peking. Through the kindness of Lucius Porter, China-born, a Yale Divinity School graduate on the faculty of the recently organized Yenching University, I met some of them, including, if my memory serves me correctly, Hu Shih, later to become a warm friend.

China had changed strikingly since 1912. The revolution which we of Yale-in-China had observed in that year had made rapid strides. What was called the May Fourth Movement was three years old. Begun in 1919 with Hu Shih as a leading figure, its effect was most marked among students. Sometimes called the Renaissance or New Tide, it stressed a critical examination of all knowledge, including especially China's past. As a symbol, it promoted respectable writing in a standard vernacular rather than the classical style which for many centuries had been the vehicle for all serious literature. As a symbol of the change I noted on a train two Chinese youths, a boy and girl, obviously students, holding hands, an action which ten years earlier would have been sharply condemned as immoral.

The enlarged meeting of the World's Student Christian Federation was the first since World War I. Its German delegation was led by former Chancellor Michaelis and had in it the distinguished theologian Karl Heim. Heim and I were billeted together but, with my slight knowledge at the time of technical theology, I did not fully appreciate the privilege.

A major issue which engaged the gathering was that of the Christian's attitude toward war. Prominent in the gathering was Henry T. Hodgkin, an English Quaker, formerly a medical missionary in West China, and one of the founders of the Fellowship of Reconciliation. Conflicting convictions were presented. I was appointed chairman of a committee to attempt to formulate a statement which would meet the minds of all. We submitted a report which in substance said that we must seek to remove the causes of war and so, ultimately, war itself. To this Hodgkin somewhat reluctantly assented as coming as near to his pacifist position as it would apparently be possible to bring the entire meeting. But Michaelis, speaking for the German delegation, took exception to the hope of eliminating war. He believed that the Bible teaches that war cannot be done away, that it will recur, even more disastrously, and that ultimately at the culmination of the age God will intervene and bring to an end the whole sorry human failure. In the brashness of my immaturity, and, perhaps, an example of the naïve optimism with which Continentals have charged Americans, I said that this seemed to me little short of blasphemy, for when we were taught to pray: "Thy Kingdom come; thy will be done, on earth as it is in Heaven," we were expected to have faith that the petition would be answered.

With his genius for discerning and enlisting ability, Mott sensed the promise of a young Chinese layman, T. Z. Koo, who had been prominent in arranging the mechanics of the conference. Mott now engaged him to be a secretary of the Federation, a post in which he long gave distinguished service.

The trip to China gave opportunity for a visit to Changsha. There I saw the notable strides that had been made in the ten years of my absence. An ample campus had been purchased outside the north gate of the city. As an illustration of the revolutionary changes, most of the city wall had been demolished. On the campus the best hospital in Central China had been erected by a gift of Edward Hume's Yale classmate, Edward Harkness. It was the base of the Hsiang-Ya Medical and Nursing Schools, a joint Chinese and American enterprise. Across a road and north of the hospital on its own campus, the Middle

School was housed in several buildings, including a chapel. For the staff, comfortable though not luxurious residences had been erected.

From Changsha I went to Shanghai for a meeting of the National Christian Conference. The gathering was troubled by dissensions between conservatives and non-conservatives. A Yale Divinity School graduate, the brilliant but frail T. T. Lew, attempted to bring both sides together, using a phrase: "Agree to differ, but resolve to love." Out of the Conference came the National Christian Council of China, a heartening effort at coöperation. It succeeded in enlisting not only the non-fundamentalists, but also the largest conservative body, the China Inland Mission. In it, as was proper, Chinese were given leading places.

From Shanghai, by previous arrangement, Carl Rogers and I joined forces. We went first to Manila. There the movement for independence was under way. To understand the official American attitude I obtained an interview with the Governor-General, Leonard Wood. While I was waiting in his office a charming young military aide, obviously a West Point graduate, answered my inquiries by saying, as though it was axiomatic, that some peoples are born to govern and some to be governed. Here was as succinct and frank a statement of nineteenth-century benevolent imperialism and colonialism as I had heard. When General Wood came, he was emphatic that the United States must retain its hold on the Philippines because of their strategic importance to its interests in East Asia. He illustrated his point by moving around on his flat-topped, otherwise vacant desk ink-well, penholder, and blotter, to make vivid the major countries in the area. As an appointee of the Republican administration, he took a view quite opposite to that of its predecessor, the Democrats, with their rapid promotion of self-government.

From Manila we went to Hong Kong. I made a brief side trip to Canton, to see missions, especially Canton

Christian College, and the site of the Thirteen Factories of pre-treaty days. From Canton I went to Macao for a few hours. Arriving in Hong Kong from Macao, I came down with my old enemy, amoebic dysentery. I had about a week in a Catholic hospital, undergoing a treatment different from that of 1911. Declared convalescent, but with instructions for regular injections of the curative drug, emetine, still accompanied by Rogers, I went to Swatow, where I visited the Baptist mission, and to Foochow where we had several days, seeing a noted Buddhist monastery, missions, and the new campus of Fukien Christian University. Arriving in Shanghai, I sought counsel of a friend, a graduate of the Harvard Medical School, and under his direction spent several days in a sanatorium with a new and even more drastic treatment. Released, I visited missions in Hangchow and Soochow, experiencing as always the generous hospitality of missionaries. Carl Rogers rejoined me in Shanghai and we sailed for America by way of Japan. We had several days in Tokyo, where I saw missions, called on eminent Japanese Christians, and spent a number of hours in a noted library gathering material, as I had in Shanghai, for *A History of Christian Missions in China*.

After a few weeks in my Oregon home, hopefully to complete recuperation, I returned to Yale in time for the autumn term and plunged immediately into teaching and a variety of other responsibilities. When I came to the Yale faculty I was already a member of the Board of Managers of both the American Baptist Foreign Mission Society and American Baptist Board of Education. Because of my interest in East Asia I became an early member (I think a charter member) of the Council on Foreign Relations and shared in some of its special meetings on East Asia. More important was the chairmanship of the program committee preparing for the quadrennial of the Student Volunteer Movement to be held over the year-end of 1923-1924. Previous quadrennials had been planned and chaired by Mott. During the last one with

him as its head, that in 1919-1920, some of the more
mature students had been restive under his leadership,
declaring that he did not understand either the world
situation or the student mind. Mott was moving to other
responsibilities and insisted on resigning from the Chairmanship of the Executive Committee of the Movement.
Robert Wilder, to whom the birth of the Movement was
chiefly indebted, had been persuaded to take the General
Secretaryship and Joseph Robbins, recently a missionary
in the Philippines, succeeded Mott as Chairman of the
Executive Committee. The chairmanship of the program
committee entailed frequent meetings in New York and
an attempt to frame a program which would be true to
the current world situation and the unchanging Gospel,
and speak to the student mind. Since the quadrennials
were the only national Christian student assemblies for
the United States and Canada, many insisted that their
special convictions be given a hearing. Yet the committee
was convinced that the quadrennial must hold true to the
purpose of its predecessors and present the challenge of
the world and the missionary enterprise. Because of their
long association with the Movement and their undoubted
and unsurpassed knowledge of the world scene and foreign missions, both Mott and Speer were urged to make
major addresses and accepted. The quadrennial was held
in Indianapolis. The atmosphere was electric. Critical
groups gathered in private, but only once, and then
through a student who was not connected with them,
was the floor demanded at a plenary session.

While the quadrennial was in progress, but in no way
connected with it, death came to Henry Wright. He was
in Oakham for the Christmas recess and had a hemor-
rhage in a lung that had earlier been badly damaged
through an infection contracted several years earlier
while he was nursing one of the lads of that village who
was dying of tuberculosis. His last words were: "Life here
with Christ has been wonderful; it will be richer hereaf-
ter."

After the quadrennial I was made Chairman of the Executive Committee of the Movement. Wilder earnestly sought to make the Movement responsive to the student mind and brought students on the executive committee. It was there that I first came to know Walter Judd. He was then a medical student preparing for China and had the drive which was to characterize his years in China and his later career.

In New Haven I continued my contacts with Dwight Hall and came to know some of the leaders not only in the Christian Association but as well in other activities. The temper had changed almost beyond all recognition from my student days. The kind of Bible study, indeed any voluntary Bible study such as had flourished before World War I, was impossible. Very few undergraduates would listen to a suggestion that they consider foreign missions or even the ministry as a life work. Undergraduate agitation against required chapel was vocal and shortly prevailed. In the Divinity School the situation was different. Several able students were headed for missions and others were willing to respond when the challenge was presented to them individually—as I undertook to do.

A combination of causes brought me to an extreme physical and emotional crisis. I found sleep in the dormitory difficult. One of my older colleagues, Henry Hallam ("Hal") Tweedy, kindly offered to give me room and breakfast in his quiet home. I gratefully accepted, insisting on being a paying guest. I still kept my rooms as well as my office in the Divinity School and used the former for my student group and for guests. The trip to China, the quadrennial, and the several boards and committees on which I held membership took a heavier toll than I had realized. In addition, and more of a drain, were basic questions of the faith. I had come to see something of the seamy side of ecclesiastical and official religious life and found myself wondering whether Christianity was confirmed by its fruits. What, if any, real difference

could be demonstrated between the lives of professed
Christians and agnostics in academic circles and the
world at large? Among presumably sincere Christians I
found self-seeking for position and prestige, often rationalized as orthodoxy or liberalism. Then, too, I was without a professional theological training and was a member
of a divinity school community. Issues properly considered vital were being discussed and a vocabulary employed with which, at best, I was only vaguely familiar.
On my mother's side of the family, as I have said, some,
including the most brilliant intellectually and the best
read in such subjects, had taken a reverent but agnostic
attitude toward religion. In this my mother did not share,
but I was aware of it and never had been forced to come
to grips with it. During the winter and spring of
1924-1925 I was physically very much below par. Careful
examinations in the hospital exonerated the amoebae—
except for some permanent damage to the intestinal
tract. The summer in Oregon failed to bring full restoration and reluctantly I asked for leave for the autumn
term.

During that autumn I reached a nadir, but also had
the beginning of the answer. Again and again I had
climbed mountains in the Pacific Northwest. As I grew
older I would lie in my sleeping bag under the stars,
bright and glittering in the thin air, and would wonder
whether there was anyone in that vast universe who
cared for me and my fellow human beings any more than
I cared for the ant which I crushed when it was trying to
crawl in with me for shelter. For weeks in that autumn of
1925 I realized that I was at least an agnostic and perhaps an atheist. If that attitude persisted I would, in all
honesty, have had to resign from the faculty of the Divinity School and the ministry. I can still remember almost
the precise spot in a street in Portland when, like an
illumination, the beginning of the answer flashed on me.
"Here," I said, or a voice seemed to say to me, "is my
father. He has never let me down and has always been

dependable. Unless there is Some One in the universe who is at least as dependable and as intelligent as he, by whatever means he has been brought into being, the universe does not make sense. All our science is based on the conviction that we live in a universe, not chaos."

Of course I did not stop there. I could think of scores of others, including my mother, who were equally dependable. Later and repeatedly my friend, colleague, and fellow Baptist, William Lyon ("Billy") Phelps, prominent as a teacher of English, said from the pulpit: "The great question of life is, is God as good as Jesus?" At the time, with my historical training and the questions raised by specialists in the New Testament, I was far from certain that we could know much about Jesus. However, as time passed and I continued to listen to my colleagues, to read their books and the books by other specialists, I ceased to wonder whether knowledge of their fields would make the Christian faith untenable. I came to know men and women, both in humble walks of life and in high ecclesiastical and academic posts, who clearly bore "the fruits of the Spirit" and under great stress both maintained their Christian faith and grew it in. I found—or was found by—sufficient faith to remain on the faculty of the Divinity School. Not immediately, but as the months and years passed, increasingly, from experience and thought based on extensive reading, I found the Evangelical faith in which I had been reared confirmed and deepened. Increasingly I rejoiced in the Gospel—the amazing Good News—that the Creator of what to us human beings is this bewildering and unimaginably vast universe, so loved the world that He gave His only Son, that whosoever believes in Him should not perish, but have everlasting life. Everlasting life, I came to see, is not just continued existence, but a growing knowledge—not merely intellectual but wondering through trust, love, and fellowship—of Him who alone is truly God, and Jesus Christ whom He has sent. I was confirmed in my conviction that when all the best scholarship is taken into ac-

count we can know Christ as He was in the days of His
flesh. Although I became familiar with the contemporary
and recent studies of honest, competent scholars who
questioned them, I was convinced that the historical evidence confirms the virgin birth and the bodily resurrection of Christ. Increasingly I believed that the nearest
verbal approach that we human beings can come to the
great mystery is to affirm that Christ is both fully man
and fully God. Although now we see Him not, yet believ-
ing, we can "rejoice with joy unspeakable" in what the
Triune God has done and is doing through Him. This
Good News, so rich that it is stated in a variety of ways,
but always consistently, in the New Testament, is what
we always imperfect children, but children, are privileged—and commanded—to make known and to demonstrate to all mankind.

For the remaining years of my first decade on the Yale
faculty, the story can best be told topically rather than in
chronological sequence. Clearly my first and major commitment was foreign missions, and the Divinity School
was my prior obligation. I continued to give courses in
that field. The one on which I placed major emphasis
was the history of the expansion of Christianity. Since
more of our prospective missionaries were headed for
China than for any other land, I offered courses in the
religion and the history of missions in that country, and
in the history of American relations with China. Several
of my students became lifelong friends. To mention only
five. Frank W. Price, China-born and reared, later was
outstanding in education for the rural ministry in that
country, was a friend of many of the Chinese leaders in
church and civil life, was prominent in the Ecumenical
Movement, subsequent to the Communist mastery of the
mainland was many months in obtaining permission to
leave, after returning to this country held several posts,
among them the Directorship of the Missionary Research
Library in New York City, and taught and held pastorates
in Virginia. Lyman Hoover had hoped to go to the

Chinese Moslems, but the way did not open. Instead he went to China under the YMCA as a student secretary, was in "unoccupied" China during World War II, then was with the YMCA in New York City, and ended his active career on the staff of the Asia Foundation. Arthur O. Rinden served for years under the American Board in Fukien, after returning to this country was in a number of posts including the Secretaryship of Yale-in-China, and ended his active career as Secretary of the Council of Churches in Hartford, Connecticut—always with an interest in foreign missions. Although he was not in China, after a term with the American Board in the Philippines, Walter Tong contributed to missions in several capacities, eventually with the Commission on World Ministries of the United Church of Christ. In India Richard Keithahn had many years, partly with the American Board, in a unique, unusually self-denying mission and as a friend of Gandhi and of other but less famous deeply religious non-Christian spirits. Carl Dille was for years in Angola under the American Board and remained in the difficult 1960's when the Portuguese authorities placed increasing restrictions on Protestants.

As part of my academic functions, I became a member of the Department of Religion in the Graduate School. This department, organized and chaired by Douglas C. Macintosh of the Divinity School faculty after what he had seen at the University of Chicago, where he had taken his doctorate, was a device by which Yale graduates and students could enroll for and, hopefully, obtain an M. A. or Ph. D. As will appear later, it occupied a large part in my Yale years.

Yale-in-China continued to be a major concern. As chairman of its personnel committee I helped to obtain long-term members of the staff and "bachelors" who, on graduation from Yale College, went out, at first usually for one year at their own expense, and latterly for two

years under salary from the Yale-in-China Association—
as the Yale Foreign Missionary Society was renamed.

Because of the proximity of New York, for years I
averaged a trip a week to that city, usually on some board
or committee connected with missions. Because of my ill
health in 1924-1925, I asked to be relieved of the Chairmanship of the Executive Committee of the Student
Volunteer Movement and for two or three years resigned
from the Board of the American Baptist Foreign Mission
Society. But after a brief interval I renewed my membership on the latter and, with the exception of a one-year
term as President of the American Baptist Foreign Mission Society, was on the board until in my sixties I
believed it wise to ask that I not be reëlected to make
room for a younger man. The Foreign Missions Conference of North America and its committees took time.

The connection which longest continued and which
proved quite invaluable was an informal group which for
years bore the name of IRM—*The International Review
of Missions*—but later, to avoid any suspicion of being
official, was christened LM, presumably *Lux Mundi*. It
was begun by and long had as its sole officer A. Living-
ston ("Liv") Warnshuis. He had been a missionary in China, and, with J. H. Oldham, was one of the two initial
secretaries of the International Missionary Council. An
able administrator, with vision and initiative, after a time
in London he was transferred to New York to be in
charge of the North American office of the then youth-
ful Council. Partly because he had been a member
of a similar informal fellowship in London, early in his
American service he brought together a group of about a
dozen secretaries of mission boards and professors of
missions. Its ostensible purpose was to stimulate the
preparation of articles for *The International Review of
Missions*. That periodical was begun and long edited by
Oldham with the purpose of making it outstanding as a
comprehensive, scholarly, and stimulating medium of

thought on foreign missions. During my Denison days I had written for it. The IRM group met off-the-record over a weekend three times a year. I was a charter member and outlived all the others. As the original members retired or died, the group was recruited from younger men— to whom women were later added. Although the size increased, those asked to join were all professionally connected with foreign missions, mostly as administrators and several as scholars. After the World Council of Churches was formed, some were asked because of their connection with it or, when in the United States, were invited to its sessions. But always the primary emphasis was the world mission. When these lines were penned, I still regularly attended.

We first met in a Methodist conference center on the Hudson and then, for several years, in the Hotel Gramatan in Bronxville or in Yale. At the beginning and for many years the most vocal members were Warnshuis, Ralph Diffendorfer, of the Methodist Board, and Charles Fahs, Director of the Missionary Research Library. That library was begun at Mott's initiative after the World Missionary Conference of Edinburgh, 1910, by a generous gift of the Rockefellers. The group discussed the most burning issues of foreign missions and with utter frankness. Since I was about the only member who actually wrote for the IRM, in 1928, after the Jerusalem meeting of the International Missionary Council, I became the American correspondent of the *Review* and at the present writing still am listed in that post. At each meeting I continued to ask suggestions for articles for the IRM and passed them on to the editors.

Early in the summer of 1930 I met at Williamstown, Massachusetts, with a representative committee of the International Missionary Council. Mott presided. About fifty were present, chiefly from North America, the British Isles, and the Continent of Europe. There I met several old friends and formed a number of new friendships. Prominent among the latter was William Paton. Paton was an Oxford graduate, had been prominent in the Student Christian Movement of Great Britain and Ireland, had made an extraordinary contribution in the initial years of the National Christian Council of India, and had followed Oldham as editor of *The International Review of Missions*. He was extremely able as an administrator, was a competent scholar, was deeply committed to the world mission, and soon was outstanding in other phases of the Ecumenical Movement. We entered into a friendship which lasted throughout the rest of his all-too-brief life. At the Williamstown gathering I suggested that the IMC form a committee to promote research in missions. Out of it came an informal group and eventually a formal committee of which I was long chairman.

In February, 1929, Macmillan published *A History of Christian Missions in China*. A book of 930 pages with thousands of footnotes and covering all branches of the Church, it was long the standard, comprehensive treatment of its subject. The publishers gave it ample promotion and the Society for Promoting Christian Knowledge bought sheets and in London brought it out under its imprint. I was especially pleased by the cordial reception given by Catholics. In collecting material I had visited centers of Catholic missions in the United States. Among them was the American headquarters of the Society of the Divine Word, at Techny, on the outskirts of Chicago. There I formed a friendship with Bruno Hagspiel which continued until his death. He had travelled widely in several mission fields and had written perceptive accounts of them. I also called at Maryknoll, on the Hudson, the headquarters of the Catholic Foreign Mission Society of America. At that time the majority of the graduates were going to China. John J. Considine of their staff was an early acquaintance who became a warm friend. As will appear later, in many ways I am deeply indebted to him. A priest of complete commitment to Christ, asking nothing for himself, possessed of an amazing knowledge of missions, with wide-ranging vision and great wisdom, few if any of his generation have made greater contributions to the foreign missions of the American branch of his church. Within a few months of its publication I was pleased to find that the entire *History of Christian Missions in China* had been read aloud at meals to the student body at Maryknoll.

The first decade on the Yale faculty had other developments in path-breaking. This was in Far Eastern, especially Chinese studies. When, in 1927, Professor Williams became emeritus, at the instance of Charles Seymour, of the History Department, his title and teaching responsibilities were added to mine. I became D. Willis James Professor of Missions and Oriental History. The original suggestion was that the title be Oriental History and Missions, but I insisted on the order that would place missions first. That was chiefly because missions were my major interest. It was also because I knew that if I were to put Oriental history first I would have to give my major attention to that field and become better equipped in it, especially linguistically. As one of the few in the United States of that time with some competence in the history of the Far East, and particularly of China, I could make a contribution, but when, as I hoped, younger and more competent men arose I would not be needed. The Chinese have a saying: "In the land of the blind, the man with one eye is king." For a time, with my one eye I could help, but others with two good eyes would eventually make me superfluous. For about twenty years I taught all that was being given at Yale on China, and with the exception of research guidance in the history of Japan to a few graduate students by the superb specialist Asakawa, I offered all in the University on the Far East. In alternate years I had two survey courses, one on the history of the Far East and one on the history of China. I opened them to the entire University—undergraduates, Divinity School students, and graduate students. Most of the elections, seldom numerous, were by undergraduates.

Deeply concerned that Yale should do more, I besieged successive chairmen of the History Department and Presidents. President Angell was sympathetic and suggested that I bring together a group from schools and departments which might be expected to offer work in the field and through them formulate a plan for the entire University. I complied and the group met from time to time. After he took office, President Seymour went further and made the group a formal committee of the Faculty of Arts and Sciences. We prepared a comprehensive plan. President Seymour later told me that the existence of the plan aided him in obtaining the approval from the Yale Corporation of the appointment of George Kennedy in the field of linguistics for the teaching of Chinese. Superbly equipped, George Kennedy formulated a system for teaching Chinese which some years later became the basis for the Chinese branch of the Yale Institute of Far Eastern Languages and was widely adopted elsewhere for teaching the language to members of the armed forces and to missionaries.

Through Mortimer Graves of the American Council of Learned Societies a Committee on the Promotion of Chinese Studies was organized with the object suggested by its title. Bertold Laufer, European trained and at that time the most eminent sinologist in the United States, accepted the chairmanship. I was asked to be one of the original members. Laufer had been chiefly responsible for the notable collection of Chinese antiquities in the Field Museum of Natural History in Chicago and was the author of numerous monographs, particularly on intercultural contacts before the nineteenth century between the Chinese and other peoples. Theoretically the American Oriental Society included East Asia in its purview, but it was not concerned with recent history and stressed studies using the languages. Laufer arranged to have a special program on China in connection with and immediately before the annual meeting of the Society. Because of my pressure on the Society to do more on East Asia, I had been made a director of that organization. Following Laufer's precedent, in connection with an annual meeting of the AOS at Princeton I arranged a program at which J. J. L. Duyvendak, Professor at Leyden and a noted sinologist just coming into wide recognition, made the major address. We entered into a warm friendship which was terminated only by his death in middle life hastened by hardships suffered during the German occupation of the Netherlands during World War II. On Laufer's death, in 1930, Arthur Hummel was made chairman of the Committee on the Promotion of Chinese Studies. Formerly an American Board missionary in Shansi and a teacher in Peking he had become an outstanding master of Chinese and was chief of the Division of Orientalia in the Library of Congress.

During these years, I first made the acquaintance of Paul Pelliot, the outstanding French sinologist of the day, and had him as my guest. I was over-awed by him and his vast learning, but he was courteous and understanding.

A further contribution to the promotion of Chinese studies was through the coöperation of Lucius Porter. I dreamed of seeing an American academy of Chinese studies in Peking, somewhat after the pattern of the American Academies in Rome and Athens. It occurred to me to approach Dorothy Whitney Straight, widow of Willard Straight, who had had a distinguished career in promoting American interests in Manchuria. From the Whitney family, Mrs. Straight was heiress of a large fortune. She was noted for her generosity. At the time Lucius Porter was teaching in Columbia University. To continue his teaching at Yenching, he declined a permanent appointment at Columbia. Indeed, before asking me to Beach's chair, the Divinity School faculty had approached him and, on the same grounds, he had refused to have his name used. He made the appointment with Mrs. Straight. He and I went together and presented our plea. At my instance Lucius did most of the talking. Mrs.

Straight explained that she did not believe in endowments, but she promised a substantial sum to make possible an initial fellowship. Since we did not have the staff
for administering it, Lucius and I asked Stephen P. Dug-
gan, of the Institute of International Education, to assume the responsibility. He kindly agreed. C. W. Young
was appointed and before his early death did notable
studies on Manchuria. After the expiration of the first
grant, since Lucius was in China, I again approached the
generous donor. She renewed the scholarship. It was
awarded to L. Carrington Goodrich. Of missionary parentage, he had been reared in China and wished to specialize in Chinese studies. The fellowship made possible
residence in Peking further to develop his competence in
the field. Eventually he was Professor of Chinese in
Columbia University and in that chair had a notable
career in teaching and scholarship.

Partly because of my publishing connection with
Macmillan, in the 1920's a representative of the firm
asked me to prepare a major work on the history of
China. Since a need seemed to exist, I agreed. *The
Chinese: Their History and Culture* was the result. First
issued in two volumes in 1934, a third thorough revision
appeared in 1964. The writing of the first edition ab-
sorbed several years of writing time and entailed extensive research in the prodigious materials in Western languages—in translations, monographs, and periodicals.
Fortunately most of what I needed was in the Yale libraries. In addition to being a comprehensive treatment
of the subject it proved to be useful for its extensive
selected bibliographies and an index of Chinese charac-
ters for every Chinese word and name in the text. I had
found the latter useful in my own initial studies in the
field and no other book of a similar purpose was equipped
in that fashion. It quickly became standard.

In connection with my interest in furthering Chinese
studies I was host to T'ai Hsü, the eminent Chinese Buddhist monk who was furthering a revival of that faith

among his fellow countrymen. Attired in his formal robe, he lectured, through an interpreter, in the chapel of the Divinity School.

Other developments in the first decade on the Yale faculty had to do with international relations. Partly because of the post-World War I global situation I felt constrained to give major attention to the subject. Shortly after my arrival I gave careful study to the subject of pacifism. During the war Fay Campbell and Roland Bainton had been pacifists. The subject was being discussed by the students of the Divinity School. After much thought I became a Christian pacifist and joined the Fellowship of Reconciliation. As the name of that organization indicates, it holds that Christian pacifism requires positive action and not simply a negative attitude. Membership in the Council of Foreign Relations was a partial answer to the challenge. Early I became a member of the Federal Council of Churches' Committee on International Justice and Goodwill. In March, 1928, I organized and became the sole officer of an informal group in New Haven of faculty and townsmen on international relations. The purpose was to bring together for information and discussion leading citizens in the city and members of the Yale faculty specializing in foreign affairs. We dined together about once a month during the academic year, sometimes in the home of one of the members, at other times in a club. Often we had a guest speaker from out of town. Usually the paper was by one of our own number. We continued for about eighteen years—until I became too engrossed in other responsibilities to act as convener. Our membership included, among others, the Federal Judge, Carroll C. Hincks (who had led one of the Bible groups in the class of 1911); a leading banker, George J. Bassett; President Angell; the future President, Whitney Griswold; E. S. Furniss, Dean of the Graduate School and Provost; E. M. Borchard, Professor of International Law (brilliant, charming, very pessimistic over the international situation and eventually dying in melancholia);

Nicholas Spykman, of Dutch birth and rearing, an early professor of international relations in Yale (a superb lecturer who died early); C. E. A. Winslow, Professor of Public Health; Samuel F. Bemis, specialist in the history of the foreign relations of the United States; Ellsworth Huntington, a geographer fertile in provocative ideas; and Arnold Wolfers, in this country as a refugee from Nazi Germany, and outstanding on the faculty in international relations.

My chief interest continued to be students, undergraduates and those in the Divinity School. I brought my membership to Calvary Baptist Church, but told successive pastors that my ministry must be chiefly on the campus and to students. Students went with me on walks, short and long. I took many to dinner, some, especially freshmen, to Morey's, where I became a life member (in prohibition days, when no liquor was served). For years I had a Bible class for freshmen in Dwight Hall. While a resident secretary in Dwight Hall, Anson Stokes, eventually Bishop of Massachusetts, was the convener. The enrollment was always small. For many years I was on the board of the Yale Hope Mission and was briefly its chairman. That institution, begun in my student days by John Magee and William Borden, was an attempt to engage undergraduates in active participation in a rescue mission. For a number of years the inner group in Dwight Hall, shepherded by Fay Campbell, met weekly in my rooms in the Divinity School.

During the 1920's Christian conviction and commitment among Yale undergraduates—and, I gather, in many other universities—dwindled. At its lowest point, near the end of the decade, the attitude of even most of the officers of Dwight Hall was that Christianity is interesting, if true. Concern for foreign missions was almost non-existent. In my student days an organization existed among the colleges of the Connecticut Valley which each year had a conference on the subject. By the time I came

on the Yale faculty, it was moribund. An effort was made
to resuscitate it, but only with transient success.

Yet in the dreariest years some able undergraduates
were unashamedly Christian. Several went into the ministry. A few prepared for foreign missions and in their
maturity made outstanding contributions. Anson Stokes,
to whom I have referred, entered Yale headed for the
ministry and never wavered in his purpose. "Jerry"
Voorhis was unabashedly Christian. From an affluent
home, as an undergraduate he sought to live with the
underprivileged in New Haven. After graduation he gave
himself to the problems of boys. In the 1930's he served
in the House of Representatives, where he won the respect of his colleagues and President Roosevelt for his
integrity and adherence to high ideals. Eventually he was
swept out of office by Nixon but continued to spend
himself for others. Luther Tucker, reared in wealth, was
humorous but uncompromising in his Christian faith,
served in East Asia with the World's Student Christian
Federation, eventually followed Fay Campbell as Secretary of Dwight Hall, and for years was pastor of a congregation in a Cincinnati suburb where, with the consent of
his bishop, he celebrated communion not only according
to the Book of Common Prayer but as well, in other
services, followed the Presbyterian order. Gardiner Day
was for many years rector of Christ Church on the edge
of the Harvard Yard and a member of the Yale Corporation. James Stringham graduated from Yale College and
the Medical School and was for years a Presbyterian
missionary in China. After returning to this country and
practising for a number of years, in late middle life he
and his wife went to India, where both served the emo-
tionally distressed by prayer and psychological tech-
niques. Winston Pettus, son of a distinguished YMCA
secretary in China, graduated from Yale College and the
Medical School, became the Yale-in-China representative
on the Hsiang-Ya hospital and medical school staff and
crashed on a mountain peak when he was making a solo

flight to bring a small Army Air Corps plane with supplies
to Changsha. Theodore C. Hume, son of Edward Hume of
Yale-in-China, was pastor of the church which served the
Claremont Colleges and during World War II was shot
down when flying to Geneva to serve in connection with
the World Council of Churches (then officially described
as "in process of formation"). Kenneth B. Anthony was
on a short-term appointment in Yale-in-China, was pastor
of Congregational churches, and eventually was on the
staff of the United Church of Christ's Commission on
World Ministries. All these men I knew well during their
undergraduate days and have been happy to count them
as friends in subsequent years. They are only a few
among others, most of whom did not go into the ministry
or missions, but who in other ways gave notable service
as Christians. I cannot claim to have been responsible for
them or their accomplishments, but their friendship, begun in their undergraduate days, has been one of the
high privileges of life.

During the decade I directed a few graduate students
in their successful candidacy for the Ph. D. The first was
Elgin Moyer, who was many years a useful member of
the faculty of the Moody Bible Institute. Another was L.
C. George Paik, a Korean. A first generation Christian, he
had recurring difficulties with the Japanese because of
his suspected connection with nationalistic movements.
After World War II he was for a time President of Yon-
sei, the leading Christian university in the country.
Then, briefly and from a sense of duty, he was in a
prominent post in the government of the Republic of
Korea, and soon, in the stormy shifts in the political
scene, was temporarily forced out of that country to the
United States.

A movement with which I had no special connection
but which enlisted a few undergraduates of those years
was what was called at its several stages the First Century Christian Fellowship, the Oxford Groups, and Moral
Rearmament. I met Frank Buchman, its founder, the

year I was travelling for the Student Volunteer Movement. He was then Secretary of the YMCA in Pennsylvania State College and the movement had not yet begun. It never gained a strong footing at Yale, although for a winter in the 1920's some of its leaders lived in a home in New Haven of a Yale graduate who, with his family, was abroad for the year. Sherwood Day, Yale 1911, was briefly a secretary in Dwight Hall and was for years on the inner circle of the movement. Two Yale graduates of the 1920's whom I knew well in their student days, both clergymen, Brewster Bingham, son of a United States Senator, and Norman Schwab, son of a former head librarian of Yale, were long with the movement. I had several other good friends who were intimately associated with Buchman, but my direct contacts with him and his associates were infrequent and slight.

One of the most important friendships which began in that first Yale faculty decade was with Mrs. Charles T. Lincoln. She and her husband were long active in Calvary Baptist Church where both had Sunday School classes. A skilled typist and stenographer, she had served Dean Wright, Dean Phillips of the Graduate School, and Henry Wright. At Henry Wright's suggestion, she became my secretary. For many years she took my letters. Into 1964 she typed practically all my books. My debt to her can never be put into words.

Difficult though they were, the first ten years on the Yale faculty were extraordinarily rich in friendships and a questioned but deepening faith.

CHAPTER VII

TWENTY-TWO YALE FACULTY YEARS IN AN INCREASINGLY DIVERSE SETTING

After my first ten years on the Yale faculty the environment under which I lived changed drastically, although by stages, both physically and in personal relations. Shortly before the close of the decade Dean Brown became emeritus and was succeeded by Luther A. Weigle. Dean Brown was a noted preacher and that, when he came to the Divinity School, was much needed. As I have said, he markedly increased the enrollment and attracted a denominationally more varied student body. Dean Weigle had many gifts. In addition to being a great teacher, he was an educator, a scholar of varied and eminent attainments, and a superb administrator. He quickly stiffened the standards of admission. For a time this reduced the attendance, but it distinctly augmented the quality of the student body. He also added to the faculty, bringing on it such men as Robert Calhoun and Richard Niebuhr. The better standards and the fame of the young, promising faculty eventually brought even more students than before he came into office.

Physically the environment was completely altered. In the summer of 1931 the buildings which had been erected for the Divinity School between fifty and sixty years earlier were razed to make way for Calhoun College, one of the ten new undergraduate colleges which were erected in a revolutionary change in Yale's undergraduate housing. Money and the site had been obtained for a much enlarged plant for the School, but it would not be ready for occupancy until the autumn of 1932. In the twelve months' interval the School was housed in Hendrie Hall, formerly used by the Law School, and adjacent former residences owned by the University were assigned as dormitories.

The new Divinity School Quadrangle was one of the early achievements of Dean Weigle. By wise negotiations he had obtained a grant from the Sterling trustees for their erection and equipment. After World War I the estate of John W. Sterling had come to Yale. Sterling was a graduate of Yale College, a New York lawyer, and a bachelor. By wise investments he had acquired a fortune from which Yale eventually received about thirty million dollars. By his will most of his estate was to go to Yale. He did not give it directly, but appointed as trustees a group of his friends to whom, with some restrictions, was left the decision as to how it was to be spent. The will directed that an important building be erected as a memorial. That, at the request of the University authorities, the trustees decided should be the library, greatly needed, and in due course it was constructed. The College and the Law and Medical Schools were given buildings. But the trustees said that Mr. Sterling was not interested in religion and refused to do anything for the Divinity School. By ample endowments they created Sterling professorships which, at the decision of the President, not of the Corporation as was the rule for other appointments, were to be given to the outstanding scholars on the faculty to encourage and aid research. The trustees declined to assign one to the Divinity School. President Angell obtained one for Weigle on the ground that the latter's chair was religious education, and in approaching the trustees stressed education.

Dean Weigle went to Anson Stokes, father of the future bishop, who was a clergyman and had been Secretary of the University for more than twenty years. Mr. Stokes had talked repeatedly with Mr. Sterling about his plans for Yale and said that the latter was deeply interested in religion, but wished it to be non-sectarian. Dean Weigle pointed out that the Divinity School met that requirement, for, like the University, while originally Congregational, for several decades, along with the University as a whole, it had been officially declared to be undenominational. His request was given additional weight by the fact that, through Professor Tweedy's characteristically quiet initiative, the Rockefellers had promised a million dollars to the Divinity School on condition that it be matched from other sources. A third of the pledge had been met by the Divinity School's share in the twenty million dollar fund raised by Yale soon after World War I. That left two-thirds of a million not yet covered. The Sterling trustees promised to erect and equip the new plant from what remained of the original bequest. The two-thirds of a million dollars were, therefore, added to the endowment of the Divinity School, thus relieving the University from part of the budget of the School not covered by the income the funds' donors had given specifically for it, and which was annually made up from the income from general University funds.

The site first assigned for the new quadrangle was not far from the center of the University, a plot facing Hillhouse Avenue and occupied by two residences which belonged to Yale. The tenant of one of these houses was highly indignant at having to move and by her protests embarrassed the administration. The architect had drawn preliminary plans for the new buildings when a much larger site on the crest of a hill about a mile from the University center became available through the death of the owner. George P. Day, the Treasurer of the University and to whom the occupant of the originally assigned site had repeatedly complained, obtained an option on the other site, explained the situation to the faculty of the Divinity School, and the latter voted to endorse the change. Fortunately construction had not yet begun. The architect's plans were adjusted and enlarged to meet the new situation and in the year 1931-1932 the quadrangle bearing the Sterling name was erected. In the course of the years the change proved advantageous. The enrollment of the Divinity School grew beyond what had been anticipated and the site originally assigned would have cramped the School. Additional land in the neighborhood might have been acquired, but physical unity would have been handicapped by intervening streets. As the use of automobiles mounted, parking space would have been difficult to obtain and the distance from the University center became less important. In their later years I was glad to thank both the protesting woman and George Day for the change.

During the year in the temporary quarters, I found the space assigned me for living quarters unsatisfactory and rented a room with Professor Bacon about a mile from the School. There I slept and had breakfasts. The arrangement was happy. Professor Bacon had become emeritus and his wife was an invalid who never left her room. The additional income helped the family budget. My host was not only a great scholar, but was as well a most gracious gentlemen. Each morning as I came to breakfast he would welcome me with an outstretched hand. He had a bad heart and eventually died of an attack. I was with him at the end but retained my room until Mrs. Bacon's death a few months later. In the new quadrangle I chose a suite of two rooms undisturbed by dormitory noises. I was given an office in the commodious new building erected for the Day Missions Library, and held it until I became emeritus.

As in the preceding chapter, the story becomes less confusing if it is told topically.

After my trip to China in 1922 and its aftermath only three times before I became emeritus was I seriously troubled by ill health, and then not by the complications of my first decade. In the autumn of 1936 I came down with what proved to be typhoid, although I had repeatedly been vaccinated against it. Late in December, 1938, during an epidemic of influenza, I had a virus pneumonia which cost me a few weeks in bed. In the three illnesses, as in all my medical care in New Haven into the mid-1950's when he closed his office and retired from practice, I was deeply indebted to Arthur Bliss Dayton. We had known each other since our student days, he was a trustee of Yale-in-China, for some years was the chairman of its board, and for a time had been on its medical staff in Changsha. Since when pneumonia came the hospitals were full, he took me to his own home and had a nurse come in each day to give me such care as was required. The third time was as I was becoming emeritus and of that I will speak in the next chapter. I may add that for years while in Oregon City during vacations from Yale, my sister, Ruth, an osteopath, and her husband, W. Ross Eaton, with an M. D. from the University of Michigan, ably gave me such medical treatment as was required.

As is proper in view of my obligations, next must come my teaching and other academic responsibilities. My major course continued to be the history of the expansion of Christianity. Since it embodied much of my conception of church history—that it should cover the impact of the Gospel on all mankind and in all ages and cover all branches of Christianity—the faculty permitted it to be an alternative to the general introductory survey of church history given by Roland Bainton. As a result I had a fairly large election. Also with a substantial enrollment was a survey course on the contemporary situation in foreign missions, the relations of Christianity with non-Christian religions, and the basic reasons for the missionary enterprise. These two courses I gave each year. For any headed for China I offered the religions of China, but not every year. For most of the years I alternated the history of China and the history of the Far East, open to students in any school in the University. After World War II it was elected by some returning veterans who had been in China and by several prospective missionaries in the Institute of Far Eastern Languages. Through the latter channel the first contacts were had with several who became fast friends. Outstanding among them was David Stowe, who eventually was head of the Division of Foreign Missions, soon enlarged as the Division of Overseas Ministries, of the National Council of Churches.

Out of my involvement in foreign affairs came a course on Christianity and international relations. Similarly, because of growing participation in the field, I gave a course on the Ecumenical Movement. In both subjects I was breaking new ground at Yale. When, as I had long urged, not because of my initiative but because of the growing imperative of the world situation, more work was offered on China and East Asia by the Departments of History and Political Science, I discontinued what I had long been teaching undergraduates in these subjects and, from a growing conviction of which I will speak later, in the last years before I became emeritus I offered to undergraduates a survey of the history of Christianity. Because some in the Divinity and Graduate Schools wished it, I added to my load a reading course on one or another phase of the history of China.

When I was in my fifties, Douglas Macintosh insisted on being relieved of the chairmanship of the Department of Religion. The men teaching in the field asked me to take on the burden. I reminded them that in most of the subjects with which they dealt I had at best only a slight acquaintance and could not hope, as had Macintosh, to give expert advice to students majoring in them. I said that if they would each take responsibility for such supervision as fell within their respective fields, I would be willing to be the coördinating officer. They agreed, and I became the channel between the Department and the administration of the Graduate School, was for years a member of that School's Board of Permanent Officers, and smoothed out the tangles inevitable in any academic post of that kind. Later, because Sidney Lovett, Chaplain of the University, wished a larger undergraduate offering of courses in religion, the Department was reorganized somewhat on the pattern of several other departments, with undergraduate and graduate sections. One of my colleagues who under the new arrangement offered courses in religion to undergraduates was made chairman, and I became Director of Graduate Studies with the same duties as before. In that position I served until I became emeritus.

When in 1949 Dean Weigle retired, still the sole Sterling Professor on the Divinity School faculty, he suggested to President Seymour that I be given that rank. Seymour said that he had already decided to take that action and at once wrote me of the appointment. It was a pleasant recognition but brought no additional duties.

As earlier, a major interest was in those preparing for foreign missionary service. The Divinity School did not have many in any one year with that objective. Some matriculated when they were undecided and during their years at Yale came to a clear conviction. A full list would unduly prolong these pages. As I write, some names quickly rise to memory. I think of Tracy Jones, son of a YMCA secretary in China, who entered Yale quite undecided vocationally. While there, a purpose came, assisted by a fellow student whom he courted and who was positive in her objective. They served in China, were compelled by the Communist mastery of the mainland to leave, and for a time were transferred to Malaya. He was then asked to share in administration and promotion in the United States. Eventually he became the head of the foreign section of the Methodist board of missions and grew to be, in the best sense of that word, a missionary statesman. Newton Thurber, whom I first knew as a Yale undergraduate and then when he came to the Divinity School, for years was in Japan, on one furlough was Secretary of the Student Volunteer Movement, and in that post organized and administered a quadrennial convention. Returning to Japan he was assigned to administration and later, reluctantly but from a sense of duty, became the East Asia secretary of his board, the United Presbyterian Church's Commission on Ecumenical Mission and Relations. Living in an adjoining apartment with the Thurbers in his Divinity School days and also a graduate of Yale College was Keith Bridston. Later he was with the British Student Christian Movement, the World's Student Christian Federation in Europe, taught in theological schools in Indonesia, was the executive officer of the Commission on Faith and Order of the World Council of Churches, and after an intensive study of a phase of theological education in the United States, taught theology in the Lutheran seminary in Berkeley. Robbins Strong, reared in Geneva where his father was long on the staff of the World's Committee of the YMCA, came to the Divinity School from Oberlin, went to China under the American Board, during the American involvement in World War II was with his family interned in Wei Hsien, after repatriation returned to China with the YMCA, was transferred first to Paris with a special Russian assignment, then to the World's Committee in Geneva, and later was on the New York staff of the United Church of Christ's Commission on World Ministries. Philip Williams was first thinking of medical missions, then, marrying "Tinker," a student in the Divinity School, enrolled in that School, and with her had years in Japan. Frank Cooley went to China under the YMCA, was unusually close to students, after the Communist seizure of the mainland was the last of the YMCA foreign secretaries to be given an exit permit, for a year was in what was equivalent to solitary confinement, on release came again to the Divinity School, and after further work went to Indonesia under the Presbyterians. Hal and Helen Shorrock met in the Divinity School. They went to Japan under the Disciples of Christ. Later Hal was sent to Korea to aid in the administration of relief. He next served in

Geneva in a similar capacity, but on a global scale. He then was made responsible for the financial administration of the International Christian University in Tokyo. Creighton ("Corky") B. Lacy was China-born and reared, for a time was in China with the Methodists, and eventually was Professor of World Christianity in Duke University. Lawrence Henderson went to Angola under the American Board. There he served effectively during the mounting tensions which the Portuguese regime imposed on Protestants. John Heinrichs had years in Southern Rhodesia in its tense racial situation. Norman Thomas, whom I first had in class as an undergraduate, after graduating from the Divinity School and some years in a pastorate in Oregon, also went to Southern Rhodesia and remained there after it became simply Rhodesia. Henry Leiper, China-born, son of Henry Smith Leiper whom I had first met when he was a freshman in Amherst when I was travelling for the Student Volunteer Movement and for some years was a missionary in China, returned to the land of his nativity, left after the Communists mastered the mainland, became pastor to Presbyterian students at the University of California and then Pennsylvania State College, and died of an unusually painful cancer. A radiant spirit, even in his last days when heavy sedation could not prevent acute suffering, he was an inspiration to callers and to his children. James Alter, of India missionary parentage, after his Yale undergraduate course, came to the Divinity School. In spite of chronic severe diabetes, by proper medication he learned to live with it, and directed a unique enterprise in India. His brother Robert matriculated in the Divinity School during my last years of teaching and after graduating went to India. Daniel D. Allen, from Yale College, became a close friend in the Divinity School and went to India where he served in several capacities. Robert Marble had years in India in a village setting, and then moved into famine relief. Reid Graham as principal of a theological school at Poona helped that institution to grow in physical equipment and educational standards. Clay Erickson, from Linfield, had years in Burma under the difficult post-World War II years and the mounting restrictions by the government. In 1966, with all other missionaries, by government order he was expelled from Burma. Roland Harker, who first went to Japan under the Methodists, shortly after World War II became a member of the staff of Moral Rearmament in that country.

In addition to these friends, whom I knew when they were candidates for the Bachelor of Divinity and some of them earlier as Yale undergraduates, were a number who did their doctorate under my supervision or who came to read under my direction. Among the latter was R. Pierce Beaver, who already had a Ph. D. in history from Cornell. He soon was a missionary in China. On returning to this country, forced out by the Japanese invasion, after a few years in teaching he followed Charles Fahs as Director of the Missionary Research Library. From there he went to the University of Chicago as Professor of Missions in the Divinity School and did distinguished writing as well as teaching. Before going to China, Samuel H. Moffatt, from a missionary family with an enviable record in Korea, after graduating from Wheaton College and Princeton Theological Seminary, took his doctorate at Yale under my direction. For a time he was in China and then, because of the Communist occupation, went to the land of his birth. David Gelzer had a family connection with the historic missionary seminary in Basel. Following his B. D. at Yale and teaching in the College of Idaho, he did his doctorate under me, went to Cameroon, and in time was placed in charge of the high-grade theological school instituted to raise the academic level of the ministry in that area. Charles Stokes had both his B. D. and Ph. D. from Yale, and for years served with the Methodists in Korea. Winburn Thomas, after some time in Japan, did his dissertation, later published, on a period of Protestant missions in that country. He became the Secretary of the Student Volunteer Movement, was in several centers in

East Asia, notably Jakarta, and later was with the United Presbyterian Church's Commission on Ecumenical Mission and Relations. Luther Copeland, a Southern Baptist missionary in Japan, eventually was Professor of Missions in the Southeastern Baptist Theological Seminary in Wake Forest, North Carolina.

Increasingly the organizational aspect of foreign missions claimed me. For years, as I have suggested, I continued on the Board of the American Baptist Foreign Mission Society. Various committees of the Foreign Missions Conference were time-consuming. For several years I was a member of the board which administered the Nanking Theological Seminary endowment. The Federal Council of Churches selected me for the small group which for several days in April, 1941, met at the Missions Inn in Riverside, California, with a deputation from Japan from the incipient *Kyodan* which then was being formed to forestall pressure from the government to bring together Protestants of that country under the heightening international tensions. Awake to the mounting danger of war between the United States and Japan, the frightening prospect of what some of us saw to be all but inevitable, we entered into a fellowship of prayer which remained unbroken in the tragic years after Pearl Harbor. Among the Japanese were Kozaki, a graduate of the Yale Divinity School and pastor of a Kumiai (Congregational) church in Tokyo; Kagawa, whom I had met in 1922 when he was living sacrificially in the slums of Kobe in an attempt to show Christian love to derelicts; Yuasa, with whom I was to have long association, especially when he became the first President of the International Christian University; Saito, whom I had known through the YMCA and the World's Student Christian Federation, and who after the war was to supervise the repatriation of Japanese civilians from the mainland of Asia; and Michi Kawai, a radiant Christian, daughter of a Shinto priest, and prominent in the YWCA.

I maintained connections with the Student Volunteer Movement, although not as chairman of any committee. I was at the three quadrennials that followed the one at Indianapolis which I had helped to plan. Increasingly, in the student temper of the 1920's and 1930's the traditional appeals had little force. Most of the delegates, although nominally Christian, were quite unintelligent in their supposed faith and not sufficiently committed to respond to a presentation of missions. Therefore a much more highly selective process to assure background for the world mission was employed for the quadrennial in the College of Wooster over the year-end of 1938-1939. Pneumonia prevented my attendance, but I was at the one in Toronto four years later, also smaller and more intensive, and at the two following ones in Lawrence, Kansas, and the three, after I became emeritus, in Athens, Ohio.

Official relations with the International Missionary Council multiplied. In the summer of 1932 I went to Herrnhut as an American delegate to a meeting of the Committee. Herrnhut was chosen because it was the headquarters and historic center of the Moravians, notable pioneers in Protestant foreign missions. It was a charming community on the Lusatian side of the mountain border with Czecho-Slovakia from which the original settlers had come to escape persecution. Mott presided. I was billeted with a retired bishop who had served in Surinam. On the journey to Herrnhut we passed through Dresden, not fully rebuilt after the destruction of World War I, and in Herrnhut found apprehension of the Nazi menace. While we were at Herrnhut the research committee was formally constituted and I was appointed chairman.

An incident remains vivid on which I look back with some regret. A Vice-Chairman of the Council was the Bishop of Salisbury, St. Clair George Donaldson. Each morning he had a celebration of Holy Communion. One day, in full committee, he felt his conscience impelled him to tell us that all of us were welcome, but, not very

27942

tactfully, he went on to say that he could not possibly take communion at non-Anglican celebrations. I leaned over to a white-haired lady whose husband was a minister of the Church of Scotland, and said: "If that is Christianity, I'm done." With a quiet smile she said: "It is not."

I must immediately add that a few years later a smaller committee of the IMC met as guests of Bishop Donaldson in Salisbury to plan for the enlarged meeting scheduled for the year-end of 1938-1939. A more gracious, modest host I never have had. He fully justified the Anglican designation of a bishop: "Father in God."

On the return from Herrnhut I stopped overnight in Leyden as a guest at Oegstgeest, the headquarters of the missions of the Dutch Reformed Church. There I first met Hans Hoekendijk. He was planning to be a missionary and kindly guided me around Leyden. Thus began a continuing friendship with a future leading specialist in missions.

Because of the enlarged meeting, first scheduled for Hangchow and then because of the Japanese invasion of China transferred to the Christian College at Tambaran, a suburb of Madras, several preliminary planning meetings of a small inner group were held which I attended. One was in Old Jordans, an historic Quaker rural center not far from London. Here I first met Hendrik Kraemer, who was being asked to write *The Christian Message in a Non-Christian World*, in preparation for Tambaram. Another was in Northfield, with its association with Moody. At these meetings I met many whom I was honored to call friends and from whom I learned much of the situation in various parts of the world.

Although not avowedly an answer to *Rethinking Missions* (published in 1932), Kraemer's book was generally so regarded. *Rethinking Missions* was the climax of the Laymen's Foreign Missions Inquiry, an elaborate project undertaken and financed by American laymen, with John D. Rockefeller, Jr., bearing a large proportion of the ex-

pense. It was an intelligent and honest attempt, with the
assistance of competent experts, at an appraisal of the
missions of some American denominations in Japan, China, Burma, and India. The most provocative feature was
the introductory chapter of *Rethinking Missions* written
by W. E. Hocking, a distinguished philosopher of the
Harvard faculty. It seemed to many to undercut the theological convictions on which foreign missions were based.
In that opinion I shared and gave expression to it in *The
International Review of Missions*. The position of *The
Christian Message in a Non-Christian World* was almost
the exact opposite of *Rethinking Missions*.

The major emphasis of the Tambaram gathering was
on the Church, and especially on its rootage in the non-
Occidental world. It was an attempt, in the face of the
passing of Western imperialism and colonialism, to make
missions ancillary to the churches which were growing
out of the Protestant missionary effort of the preceding
century-and-a-half. In the planning for the meeting I had
been stressing the importance of that approach, but the
global situation was such that no words of mine were
needed, and the program would doubtless have been ori-
ented with that purpose uppermost had I never uttered a
word. In accordance with the objective, something over a
majority of the delegates were from the churches founded by Protestant missionaries in lands outside Europe and
North America. This was a marked advance over the
meeting in Jerusalem in 1928 and even more strikingly in
contrast with the World Missionary Conference in Edinburgh in 1910. Protestantism and Anglicanism were becoming world-wide and not, as a prominent Anglican had
said earlier in the century, "the reaction to Christianity of
the Teutonic mind."

As a delegate from North America I was in Tambaram. There I met many old friends and made many
new ones from all six continents. Most of those whom I
had known earlier had come up through the Student
Volunteer Movement and the World's Student Christian

Federation. They were indebted to the global vision and dedication from which these fellowships had sprung and confirmed my growing conviction that to be true to the Gospel the history, contemporary status, and plans for the years ahead for missions must be viewed in terms of the entire human race. I had said as much in preliminary papers for the conference.

Because of obligations at Yale, in the journey to and from Tambaram I spent only the time needed for travel and the conference. However, through steamer and rail schedules I was able to see a little of missions, including two days and a night with my McMinnville classmate, Charles Rutherford, in the Telugu country, and the YMCA in Cairo, where Wilbert Smith, a friend from Student YMCA and Student Volunteer days was the head American secretary. In Cairo I also stood by the grave of William Borden.

From Port Said I flew to Palestine and back—the first of many thousand miles by air in later years and in many countries. A limousine took me to Jerusalem, where for a few days I was the guest of Nelson Glueck in the American School. I arrived in a period of unusually acute tension between Arabs and Jews. Palestine was under British mandate, but violence might erupt at any moment. Curfew had been imposed. When we went to Bethlehem my host was insistent that we return before early dusk could bring danger of an attack. Four memories stand out vividly from those brief days. One was the comment of Glueck, Jew though he was, that he sometimes wondered whether it would not have been better had there never been any Jews. A second was his statement from his years of archeology in Palestine that of the hundreds of pre-Christian Jewish graves which he had excavated all bore evidences of cults which competed with the worship of Jahweh—vivid evidence of the minuteness of the minority who held exclusively to the God who claimed their sole allegiance and by whom the writings of the prophets and the psalmists had been cherished and transmitted. A third, illuminating the current Jewish scene, was an evening with Judah L. Magnes, President of the Hebrew University. Radiant with a deep religious faith, he said rather shyly that in the light of the prevalent scepticism in the institution among teachers and students, to his relief and surprise he had found that some of the faculty, even though a minority, believed in God. The fourth was an opportunity to visit the magnificent YMCA building. The fruit of a dream formed in college days by Archibald C. Harte, a World Service secretary, it was an attempt to witness to Christ in a city where Jesus had taught and was crucified and over which He wept, and which, much more even than in His day, was torn by religious factions, some of which, tragically, had their rise in professed loyalty to Him. All four experiences posed profound historical and theological problems with which I was forced to wrestle, of the fashion in which God has dealt and continues to deal with us men. Here is a basic question on which I have meditated and have striven to discern the answer as I have dealt with the history of Christianity.

The India journey added to the evidence which discouraged further trips to the Orient. On my return trip, I left Madras running a high temperature from a disturbance in the intestinal tract. By the time we reached the Suez the ship's doctor had brought it back to normal, but I picked up an infection in Jerusalem which kept me on a restricted diet for a number of days.

More important was fellowship on the return voyage. One afternoon, to air the dissent of a Brazilian pastor from my statement that the Catholic Church is a Christian Church, he and I had a public discussion in the ship's lounge. His experience had been such that he declared that church to be an enemy of Christ. He did not convince me, but enabled me to come in close contact with an angle of the Latin-American scene of which I had been vaguely aware but now had forced itself on me. In the company were Minnie Soga and Hachiro Yuasa, each a striking illustration of Christian witness in current tragic conflicts. Miss Soga was a South African princess with whom I kept in contact for years. She maintained an unembittered spirit in face of *apartheid*. Out of Christian conviction Yuasa had left a safe academic post of teaching and research in the Imperial University in Kyoto to the hazardous presidency of the Doshisha, the Christian university in that city. He was forced out of office by militant nationalism and spent the war years in America.

Because of the advent of World War II soon after Tambaram, the International Missionary Council could not hold another enlarged meeting until 1947. But, significant of the vitality of that organization and the vision and faith which created and inspired it, was its contribution through "the Orphaned Missions Fund." That fund bridged the hostile lines and kept alive the global Christian fellowship by maintaining, through gifts from thousands, chiefly in Great Britain and North America, the missions separated by war from the constituencies which normally supported them. The "orphaned missions" were mostly German, and thus of an "enemy" people, and were also French and Dutch when the German occupation interrupted most of the normal contributions. The Lutheran World Federation helped—a continuing Christian fellowship across warring boundaries.

In the summer of 1947 the International Missionary Council, to renew physical contacts and to plan for the future, held a meeting on a quiet campus at Whitby, Ontario. It was not as large as that at Tambaram, but it was even more representative of the "younger churches." Following in the trend which had been mounting since Jerusalem, 1928, it described the relation between the "younger" and the "older" churches as that of "partners in obedience" to Christ's "Great Commission." With Richey Hogg, of whom I am to say more later, I wrote the official popular report under the title *Tomorrow is Here*. A few years earlier I had written a small survey of the contemporary world mission as *Missions Tomorrow*. The connection is obvious.

My last attendance at an enlarged meeting of the International Missionary Council was at Willingen in 1952. I had previously been present at a meeting of the Committee in Leyden in 1948 and, as an observer, was to be at a meeting of the Committee on Staten Island in 1954. Continuing but unofficial contacts were maintained through the LM Group.

Closely associated with my connection with the International Missionary Council was that with the World Council of Churches. In the 1930's an invitation made me a member of the American Committee on Faith and Order. Its secretary and executive was Floyd Tompkins, whom I had first met when I was travelling for the Student Volunteer Movement and who, to give more time to Faith and Order, had taken a small semi-rural parish in Washington, Connecticut. The Committee was made up chiefly of older men, some retired, who had been in the earlier stages of the movement and had been present at the notable pioneer meeting in Lausanne. They were very deliberate, so much so that "Pit" Van Dusen, who became a member about when I did, was humorously impatient and soon withdrew. I was equally impatient, and pled pressing duties as an excuse for irregular attendance.

Parallel with Faith and Order was Life and Work. Begun by Nathan Söderblom, after his death J. H. Oldham assumed responsibility and organized the notable meeting at Oxford in July, 1937, on Church, Community, and State. At his request I wrote a chapter for one of the preliminary studies. He called it rather "thin," but used it. I was asked to give one of the major addresses, chiefly, I was told, because from the historical standpoint I could bring a note of hope and offset the pessimism of some of the other speakers. Unfortunately my father's death in May brought family duties in Oregon and I had to beg off.

Following the meeting of Life and Work at Oxford and the one a few days later of Faith and Order at Edinburgh, a consultation under William Temple, then Archbishop of York, suggested bringing the two together in a world council of churches. A meeting to draft a constitution was called to convene at Utrecht in May, 1938. Officials of the Northern Baptist Convention asked me to represent them. About a hundred of us gathered in a hall in Utrecht under the chairmanship of William Temple. A large proportion of us had known one another through the World's Student Christian Federation, the Student Volunteer Movement, and the International Missionary Council. Indeed, the leadership, including Temple, had come up through the Student Christian Movements which arose from the Student Volunteer Movements in various countries and either had known one another personally or had known about the others. Temple was an ideal presiding officer, invariably courteous and intent on keeping the meeting on a high spiritual plane. The gathering was marked by unbroken harmony sobered by the international situation and the importance of our assignment. My only contributions were to suggest a process for recognition as potential members congregationally organized denominations such as Baptists and Congregationalists; and to insure the continuation of the preliminary organization in case a war delayed formal inauguration. Had I not made the latter motion a way would undoubtedly have been found to meet the emergency. But it helped to make possible what was called "the World Council of Churches in Process of Formation." William Temple was the obvious choice for the continuing Chairman. W. A. Visser t'Hooft, whom I had met earlier as an officer of the World's Student Christian Federation, was the Secretary. His service in the office was one of the outstanding achievements in the entire history of Christianity.

When, in 1948, at Amsterdam, the World Council of Churches was fully constituted, I was honored to be

present as a consultant and shared in the discussion—
although not as a voting delegate. My chief contribution,
which I pressed over-vigorously, was to point out that the
World Council of Churches, together with the International Missionary Council and other phases of the
Ecumenical Movement, was an entirely new development. I said that those who talked, as many did, of "reunion" as though union had once existed, were oblivious
of the fact that never had all those who called themselves
Christians been united and that beginning in New Testament times divisions, some of them bitter, had punctuat-
ed the history of the faith. Here, I said, is something new.
I did not convince many—perhaps any—but I am still
clear that my affirmation is backed by history.

Connected with my missionary purpose and the
Ecumenical Movement was membership in an unpubli-
cized prayer group. It was begun in 1888 at the suggestion of David McConaughy, the first American YMCA
secretary in India. I am not completely sure of all the
original membership. I know that Mott and McConaughy
were two. When, in the 1930's, I was asked to join, its
most faithful members were McConaughy, who, because
of health, seldom attended but regularly sent his "prayer
notes"; John R. Mott; Robert E. Speer; Robert P. Wilder,
who was then living in retirement in Norway but contributed his "prayer notes"; Delavan Pierson, son of Arthur T. Pierson, long editor of *The Missionary Review of
the World* and which the younger man carried on until,
because of a falling subscription list, it was discontinued;
Samuel M. Zwemer, outstanding as a missionary to the
Moslems and the founder and editor of *The Moslem
World;* John Mackay, then President of Princeton Theological Seminary and originally a missionary in Latin
America, first in Lima and later as a lecturer to intellectu-
als in several centers in that vast area, and latterly a
secretary of the Presbyterian Board of Foreign Missions;
Samuel M. Cavert, long a secretary of the Federal Coun-
cil of Churches and later chief secretary of the National

Council of Churches; and Jesse R. Wilson, formerly a missionary in Japan, then successor to Wilder as General Secretary of the Student Volunteer Movement, and at the time of his retirement a secretary of the American Baptist Foreign Mission Society. Each month we sent our "prayer notes" to our secretary, who for many years was Pierson. They included "praise" for what we were thankful to God, and "prayer" for what was uppermost in our concerns at the moment—sometimes personal appointments for the coming month, often specific issues confronting one or another phase of the world mission, and frequently features of the international situation. Pierson had these typed and circulated among us. Once a year we met for our "quiet day," usually in a New York hotel, but for several years in Zwemer's New York apartment. We knelt while each led in prayer, then, rising, summarized the main features of our past year. After lunch we told what we anticipated for the coming twelve months, especially our individual burdens and our concerns for others, and again knelt while each offered prayer. As our numbers were depleted by death or a change of residence, others were added, always because of their responsibilities in the missionary enterprise. Mott was the last survivor of the original group. In his late eighties he came to his final "quiet day," and although nearly deaf and with failing eyesight, sat through the hours without speaking.

My writing was an outgrowth of the global outreach of the Christian faith. If, as we Christians believe, the Gospel is for all men, historians with a Christian commitment must view their fields from that perspective. Even if they deal with a subject limited in time or geography, they must recognize that its setting is in the entire range of mankind's record. That is a basic conviction which underlay all my authorship. As I have suggested, even my first book, my doctoral dissertation, strove to deal with the history of the relations between the United States and China in their first sixty years in all their

aspects and in the setting of the entire range of the
history of China and its culture and of the impact of the
rest of mankind. The global stance entailed in my missionary purpose also led me into my advocacy of Far
Eastern history and my path-breaking in that phase of
the study of the history of mankind. It also governed my
teaching, first in Reed and Denison and then in Yale. As I
have said, my two major courses in the Divinity School
were a world survey of the contemporary scene and the
history of the expansion of Christianity.

The latter became the subject of my largest writing
project. It was in seven volumes. While I was at work on
the first volume, Eugene Exman, who, as I have said, as
one of my students at Denison had had the course which
had been preliminary to the series and who had recently
become head of the religious department of Harper &
Brothers, offered me a contract, with a royalty. I had
supposed that the production costs would be so heavy
that no publisher would take the books without a subsidy.
I had as yet made no effort to find one. I warned Exman
that he might lose money, but that did not deter him. I
was glad to sign the proffered document. That began an
association with Harper & Brothers, later Harper & Row,
which covered many books and, at least to the author,
was unqualifiedly happy, with a valued friendship with
Exman and his staff. Since the sale of the series averaged
about seventeen thousand copies a volume, the publishers seem not to have lost money. The first volume appeared in 1937 and the seventh in 1945.

The volumes were blazing new trails. They embraced
the entire history of the spread of Christianity from the
beginning to 1945. All branches of the Church were covered and the range was not limited to conversions of
non-Christians but covered as well the planting of churches by migration, whether in the Americas, Australia,
New Zealand, or South and North Africa. The main
questions asked, to which answers were attempted,
were: what was it that spread, varying as that did from

age to age and country by country; why did it spread; what were the effects on the environment; and what was the effect of the environment on Christianity? The entire history of Christianity was covered and from a particular angle. Strangely, no one employing such dimensions had ever ventured on the task. The text was buttressed by thousands of footnotes with references to the sources and secondary literature.

The material was assembled over many years and from libraries in several countries. The chief reliance was on the Yale libraries and especially the Day Missions Library. In writing *A History of Christian Missions in China* I had gathered much in East Asia which proved useful. Parts of two summers were spent in London in the British Museum. A large portion of the only official sabbatical leave that I had while on the Yale faculty was utilized by weeks in Rome.

I must hasten to say that apart from a formal sabbatical, the University very generously gave me leave on salary for professional trips abroad—to Utrecht to help draft the constitution of the World Council of Churches, to India for the Tambaram meeting, and for lectures in Great Britain in 1947.

While in Rome I spent mornings in the library of the Congregation for the Propagation of the Faith. *A History of Christian Missions in China* had assured Catholic experts that I was attempting to be not only fair but also irenic. The Maryknollers had a college in Rome and one of their number, Father Considine, with a fabulous knowledge of the missions of his entire church, generously made himself available.

Father (later Mgr.) Thomas J. Tobin of the Portland, Oregon, archdiocese, who was in Rome doing graduate work in canon law, had been briefed by Mgr. Hillebrand, pastor of the Catholic Church in Oregon City and whom I had known since boyhood. He early looked me up and began a friendship of many years. At Mgr. Hillebrand's suggestion, Father Tobin, at his initiative and against my feeble protests, arranged for a private audience with the Pope, Pius XI. It had as its excuse the presentation of a copy of *A History of Christian Missions in China.* Thereby I was given a little glimpse of the ceremony of such audiences. I carried away two major impressions. The first was the pomp and ceremony attached to the court of the presumed successor of a humble Galilean fisherman and vice-gerent of the Carpenter of Nazareth. No other court in Europe—or, indeed, of the entire world of the day—had as much outward display as that of the Pope. I could have imagined myself as in the court of Louis XIV. The second was the man himself. The Pope appeared to me to have the face of a dignified executive. After emerging from the audience I told Father Tobin that he seemed to me to be a courteous Christian gentleman who was badly overworked. He was then in his mid-seventies. In his youth he had been an expert Alpinist, but he now had a bad heart and had recently come through the taxing demands of Holy Year and Holy Week. Since the Pope had been decreed by the Vatican Council of 1869-1870 to be the absolute ruler of the Catholic Church, he conscientiously lived up to that responsibility and had the reputation of exercising that power. In addition he had to see thousands, mostly in group audiences, who had no more claim on him than I. After an incredibly busy working week, he presided at long official functions on Sundays.

Since I was eager to see as much as possible of the Catholic Church and its missions at headquarters, through the Maryknollers many doors were opened to consult experts on missions. Among them were the noted and charming Belgian Jesuit, Pierre Charles, with whom at his invitation I entered into a compact of prayer, and the equally charming Archbishop Hinsley, Apostolic Delegate to Africa and later, as Archbishop of Westminster, head of the English hierarchy and a Cardinal. Maryknollers also arranged to have me present at a beatification and a canonization. The latter made a great impression on me, partly because it was the most imposing ecclesiastical spectacle that I ever saw, but chiefly for an insight which it gave me into the Catholic Church. St. Peter's, the largest church edifice in Christendom, was packed for the four-hour ceremony, with the Pope officiating. Incidentally, the service was from eight in the morning until noon and culminated in high mass, which the Pope celebrated. As the rules of his church required, he did that fasting. Here was additional evidence of the physical burden which he carried. The essence of canonization, I was told, is to commend the virtues of the saint to all Christians as worthy of emulation. The canonization that morning was of a humble Bavarian lay monk. The next night I dined with the Maryknollers. They were joking about some of the amusing incidents of the preceding day. Then, when I spoke of the fact that the Catholic Church had in that striking ceremony sought to present to its members this humble layman as an ideal Christian, the young priest sitting next to me stopped his joking, looked at me straight and said: "You are completely right. If you had seen that saint in his lifetime you would not have looked at him twice. He was exactly like one of the lay brothers who waited on us at dinner. Yet the entire Church, from the Pope down, exists to make lives of that kind possible." Unintentionally I had pressed a button which revealed the inmost purpose of this young man who was soon to be a missionary, presumably in China.

The weeks in Rome contained only some of the many instances of the unfailing courtesy shown me by Catholics. For years I was a member of the Catholic Historical Association. By invitation I read papers at its annual meetings and contributed book reviews to its journal. In January, 1953, I was the only Protestant asked to participate in what I understood to have been the first attempt to bring together for consultation on common problems representatives of the various organizations in the United States which were engaged in the foreign missions of the Catholic Church. I had often raised with Father Consid-

ine the question why this had not been done, since for
more than half a century the Protestants of North America had had similar gatherings. Whether my suggestion
contributed to the calling of the conference I do not
know—and it is not important. But I was invited to this
first of a long series and met a number of experts on
missions who became fast friends.

I may add that the seven volumes were written while I
was carrying a full load of teaching and administration,
varied by frequent trips to New York for committees. I
also managed to keep up one of my informal weekly
student groups. During these years it was made up
chiefly of young men headed for foreign missions. I was
and am grateful for the strength which enabled me to
live through the ordeal—although at the time it did not
seem a burden.

The *Expansion* led me into another path-breaking adventure. I had been concerned that no adequate survey
existed which covered the entire field of what is generally
called church history. The usual introductory and sup-
posedly comprehensive courses in the subject and the
available texts majored in Western Europe and the centuries through the Reformation. They gave the impression that all since the Reformation was a kind of curtain
call, that Christianity was fading out of the human scene,
and that it never had been very important except in
Western Europe, a region which was only a small frac-
tion of the civilized world. I had repeatedly said of secu-
lar historians that with their current oblivion to East Asia
they were not aware that the world is round. Latterly
historians and history departments were becoming less
provincial. However, church historians, so it seemed to
me, were even more purblind, and with less excuse, for if
the Gospel is for all men church history must be seen in
the context of the entire globe. Moreover, I was, and am
convinced, that never has Christianity so entered into the
life of the entire race as it has in the past four centuries
and especially in the past half-century. With that convic-

tion I undertook a survey which would cover the entire story—all aspects, all branches of Christianity, and the entire globe. I planned it within physical dimensions which would be suitable for a course an entire academic year in length and also appeal to other serious readers.

The writing entailed extensive reading in phases of the story with which I had only cursory familiarity. The gap was particularly acute in the history of doctrine. Fortunately a colleague, Robert Calhoun, gave a course in the subject which stressed the pre-Reformation period, where I was especially deficient. He was rightly noted for his accuracy and lucidity. I audited it and at the same time did much reading in the field. I also made myself familiar with the standard sources and surveys on other pertinent aspects, such as monasticism, and, of course, the Eastern Churches and the United States. The writing was begun in 1948 and the volume, of 1516 pages, was published in the spring of 1953, on the eve of my entrance into the emeritus status.

Whenever occasion offered, through lectures and articles, I sought to express my convictions where they would gain a hearing with specialists. For example, in 1945 I was President of the Society of Church History, and in the address which was the chief duty of that office, I presented what I was persuaded should be the approach by its members. In 1949 I was President of a much larger and more varied body, the American Historical Association. Here my address was *The Christian Understanding of History*. As I expected, the reception was mixed, for none of my predecessors had ventured into even a remotely related area. As the meeting adjourned the Catholic priests who were present rushed up and said: "The theology was perfect." By the grapevine I heard that many of my auditors were disgusted. Some said that if they wanted to hear a talk on the subject they would go to church. However, no discourtesy was shown me. Offprints of the address—which, as were all of its predecessors and successors, was printed in the following

January number of *The American Historical Review*—
were quickly exhausted. Later through a national organization the Methodists reprinted it under the somewhat
spectacular title, *Master of the Waking World*.

Because of what I was writing, many invitations for
lectures came. Some were in theological schools and others in universities. From several of them books issued. To
name them all would unduly burden these pages. A few
which stand out in my memory can be mentioned. One
was a series under the historic Lowell Lectures. Mine
were delivered in King's Chapel in Boston. For them and
also for delivery as the Powell Lectures in the Canadian
School of Missions in Toronto, I wrote *Anno Domini*. In
the autumn of 1940 I gave the William Belden Noble
Lectures in Harvard. They appeared as *The Unquencha-
ble Light*. In connection with them during that semester I
made weekly trips to Cambridge and offered, for credit in
the College and the Graduate and Divinity Schools, my
course on the history of the expansion of Christianity.

The most extensive expedition for lectures was in the
autumn and early winter of 1947. The occasion was the
Edward Cadbury Lectures in the University of Birmingham. The small book which embodied them, *The
Christian Outlook*, was also used in seven other lecture-
ships, in the United States, all but one in theological
seminaries. Yale kindly gave me leave for the autumn
term of 1947 for my Birmingham appointment. As a
travelling companion I took Edward ("Ned") Steele, a
senior in the Divinity School and my secretary for that
year. We first went to Switzerland, partly for a brief
holiday and partly for a series of lectures in the Ecumenical Institute, in Bossey, near Geneva, a recently organized project of the World Council of Churches. We next
were in Oxford where I lectured in Regents Park College,
a Baptist theological school recently moved to that center. It used the occasion to open the lectures to the entire
University. In Birmingham we were entertained in Wood-
brook College, the Friends' unit of the Selley Oak Col-

leges. Edward Cadbury, a noted Quaker, who had endowed the lectureship, was a generous host. In addition to the series in the main center of the University, then near the heart of the city, I gave extra-mural lectures in Worcester and in the library of the Cathedral in Hereford. We had a long weekend in Cambridge as guests of Charles E. Raven, an old friend and at that time Vice-Chancellor of the University and Master of Christ's College. He arranged the customary hospitable receptions and dinners and had me give a University lecture. By then I was a Fellow of Berkeley College in Yale. Because it had a *concord amicabilis* with King's College, I dined with the King's College Fellows and was given an official place in its chapel—where, as before and in later years, I heard the remarkable boys' choir. While I was in Great Britain, I preached at a University service in St. Giles in Edinburgh and lectured in the University of Glasgow. I also lectured in the University of Manchester and to Baptists in London.

Three incidents, because of their ecumenical significance and the light that they shed for me on the Church of England, stood out vividly. One was a dinner in London arranged by a Russian Orthodox layman with a group of Anglican priests. The chairman said that they were a group which prayed for reunion under the Pope. When a few days later I asked Raven how widely representative they were, he said that I had probably seen all of them that evening. The second was with a group of bishops of the Church of England at which Geoffrey Fisher, the Archbishop of Canterbury, was present. It happened that shortly before, on the very afternoon I reached London, a service had been held in St. Martin's in the Fields, on Trafalgar Square, in connection with the inauguration of the Church of South India. The Archbishop preached the sermon and representatives of each of the coöperating English denominations had a part. In addressing the bishops I said that so great was the progress toward Christian unity such a service could not have been held twenty-five years before. That, of course, was true. But, inadvertently, I called it a service of thanksgiving. The Archbishop courteously interrupted and said: "I beg your pardon, but that designation was carefully considered. It was a service of intercession." In the Church of South India, although its bishops had received apostolic succession through the Church of India, Burma, and Ceylon, Anglican in its affiliation, clergymen ordained by their respective bodies in Britain or America and sent by their denominations to work with the new church, were accepted as clergy without Episcopal ordination. The Church of South India, therefore, was not received into communion by any of the Anglican bodies. From the standpoint of the Anglo-Catholics the Church of South India had created a fresh schism in the Body of Christ. Not all the bishops present that evening so viewed the new church, but some did, and the Archbishop would have been in for heavy criticism had he allowed my mistake to pass uncorrected. In other words, the Anglo-Catholics could pray for the Church of South India, but they could not be grateful for it. The third was in connection with a book by Ernest William Barnes, Bishop of Birmingham at the time of my lectures and whom I met. Then in his mid-seventies, that year his *The Rise of Christianity* was published. He claimed to be an Evangelical, but the book rejected the virgin birth, cast doubt on the physical resurrection and ascension of Jesus, and questioned whether at the Last Supper Christ instituted the Eucharist. Both the Archbishop of Canterbury and the Archbishop of York openly dissented from the positions taken in the book. When, a few weeks later, I was the guest of the Archbishop of York, I asked how it happened that a man of those convictions was a bishop in the Church of England. The Archbishop said with some asperity that that position had a right to be represented on the Episcopal bench.

Cyril Garbett, the Archbishop, was a man of great charm. An Anglo-Catholic, he had had a long and distinguished career as priest and as bishop in two such contrasting sees as Southwark, predominantly urban, underprivileged, and largely de-Christianized, and Winchester, prevailingly rural, where, an inveterate pedestrian, he had walked from parish to parish with a staff the head of which was shaped like a crosier. An acknowledged expert on housing, especially in slum areas, he was heard with respect whenever he spoke of the subject in the House of Lords.

One summer in the 1930's when I was gathering material in the British Museum for the *Expansion*, I had an experience which gave me an appreciative understanding of the Anglo-Catholic position. For years I had regarded the Anglo-Catholics as a narrow, snippy sect. I said to myself that such an attitude was un-Christian and far from ecumenical. An organization called the Fellowship of St. Albans and St. Sergius sought to promote understanding between the Anglo-Catholics and the Russian Orthodox. I sought an invitation to a long weekend meeting of the Fellowship, and was immediately and cordially given it. I attended joint meetings and services of the members of the two communions and in the intervals had long talks with Anglo-Catholics, both old and young. I was greeted so humbly and my questions were answered so kindly, that my prejudices melted like an iceberg in the Gulf Stream. Toward the end of the gathering I said to some of the Anglo-Catholics that so far as I could see they were at one on several features of the Church as they believed them to have existed in the early Christian centuries—as part of the Catholic or generally accepted Christian tradition, such as apostolic succession and the creeds—but on many points did not agree and recognized no central authority which could decide among them. Accordingly, so I came to believe, if they were Anglo-Catholics I and my fellow Baptists were Bapto-Catholics. We gave common assent to several features of what we held were widely accepted in the early generations of the Church—although these differed from the ones esteemed by the Anglo-Catholics—and so might regard ourselves as Catholics. But we differed among ourselves on many issues and recognized no authority whose adjudication we would accept. As I expressed this conviction—half-jokingly—most with whom I talked agreed, also smilingly. Incidentally, the weekend gave me a valued opportunity to meet and hear some of the Orthodox. Outstanding among them was Serge Nikolayevich Bulgakov, of whom I was to hear much and whom I later met more than once. After a period of scepticism he had returned to the faith of his boyhood and had become distinguished as a theologian. As another result of the weekend I was enrolled as a member of the Fellowship of St. Albans and St. Sergius, a connection which I maintained for many years.

The experiences with my own denomination were varied. By invitation I lectured in several of its theological seminaries, both North and South, and always met with courtesy. In all I came out for the Ecumenical Movement. No difficulty was encountered in the North. But Southern Baptists did not coöperate with the Federal Council of Churches, its successor, the National Council of Churches, or the World Council of Churches. Only by way of membership in the Foreign Missions Conference were they associated with the International Missionary Council. Then, in friendly fashion, they withdrew from the latter when the Foreign Missions Conference became a unit of the National Council of Churches. Yet they never raised objections to my endorsement of the Ecumenical Movement, and I was careful to recognize their conscientious dissent and urged that rather than arouse controversy and perhaps disunion in their Convention, they wait until an overwhelming consensus brought them to seek admission to the Ecumenical Movement.

Within the Northern—later the American Baptist Convention—unhappy and at times bitter debate arose, not so much over coöperation with other denominations, but over the desire of the Fundamentalists to bring the Convention to their position. The issue had arisen early in the century and had led to the withdrawal of several scores of churches to form the General Association of Regular Baptists. Soon after World War I Fundamentalists attacked what they believed to be the invasion of Baptist colleges and universities by what they described as Modernism. By then I was a member of the Board of Education, but the attack was not directed specifically against it.

On the Board of Education I sought to make my contribution through efforts to maintain the Christian character of institutions of higher education founded by Baptists but not through endeavoring to bring them to a subscription to a doctrinal statement. Since my student days in Yale I had been concerned with the seemingly inevitable drift from their moorings of colleges and universities begun by earnest Christians and embodying the Christian faith. As I had observed their history, the secularization was first in the student bodies with the enrollment of men who either were not concerned with the faith or were opposed to it. It then spread to the faculties and finally captured the trustees. I sought to suggest possible ways of reversing the trend. The Board was sympathetic, but took little action. Again and again in a variety of ways I attempted to obtain attention to the problem in more than one denomination, but with little if any success.

In the 1920's, 1930's and 1940's the Fundamentalists focussed on the Board of the American Baptist Foreign Mission Society. They charged that it was appointing missionaries who were unsound in the faith and demanded that creedal tests be applied. As a member of the Board— for after a brief withdrawal because of the ill health of the mid-1920's I had been reëlected—at almost every meeting I heard the complaints. At the annual conventions the Fundamentalists assembled before the formal opening and were vocal in their demands. The liberals associated

themselves in the Roger Williams Fellowship and stood
for what they declared to be Baptist freedom. Along with
the majority of the delegates I joined neither group. With
others in that majority I was sick at heart over the dis-
trust and seeming denial of Christian love. In time the
Fundamentalists withdrew into what bore the label of
Conservative Baptist organizations, at first for foreign
missions and later for other purposes. The annual conventions became more peaceful but the majority who
remained were conservative, although willing to coöperate with liberals on the principle that each Christian
should interpret the Bible as he believed the Holy Spirit
directed.

In May, 1951, in connection with my membership on
the Foreign Board, I went to the national convention in
Buffalo. I confined my attendance to meetings of the
Board and spent the other hours in my hotel room, working on my *History of Christianity.* Toward the end of the
Convention the telephone rang and the chairman of the
nominating committee, a graduate of the Yale Divinity
School, told me that they wished to present my name as
President for the coming year. I protested. He asked to
come to see me. I told him that I was not sufficiently a
public orator to fill the speaking engagements which
were the chief duty of the office, and that I could not be
absent from my duties at Yale for as much time as the
post required. He explained that in the cycle which had
become the Convention's tradition for the post of President—pastor, layman, woman, educator—the coming
year was the time for an educator, and that I was the
committee's choice. When I still protested, he suggested
that I call my Dean. By that time Weigle had become
emeritus and Liston Pope had the post. Liston said that
the Divinity School had a responsibility to the churches,
urged me to accept, and said that, if necessary, he would
see that my Yale load was lightened. I still demurred, but
agreed to talk with the General Secretary of the Convention, Reuben Nelson. Nelson said that in fairness the

presidential burden must be tailored to meet the other duties of the incumbent, and that if I could give the equivalent of two months that would be sufficient. I therefore gave my assent. That afternoon I was elected and presented to the Convention. I recall that I then wandered about the streets of Buffalo alone, wondering whether I would be alive twelve months later.

A few years after my tenure was over I learned, confidentially, that I had not been the nominating committee's first choice. That had been a layman, a distinguished teacher and scholar, a long-time friend of mine. After the vote of the committee was taken, one of the members, a conservative pastor, said that the man chosen was a Modernist and that, if elected, another secession from the Convention was probable. The committee reversed its action and named me.

To further better relations with the Southern Baptist Convention, my first official act was a telegram of congratulations to its newly elected President. That convention reciprocated by asking me to give a major address at their next annual meeting, in Miami, in May, 1952.

For some time discussions had been in progress of closer relations with the Disciples of Christ, looking toward possible union. At least two annual conventions had voted to meet in 1952 in the same city and on the same dates as the Disciples, to have some joint sessions, and a joint communion service. I had not been President for many days when I began to have telegrams and letters saying that if that service was held the Convention would again lose churches. During the next few months other members of our small executive committee received similar protests. Although all wished to proceed as had been planned, the committee was about equally divided as to what was wise. At the meeting in which a decision had to be reached, I said: "I will assume full responsibility. A verse in the Psalms endorses him 'who sweareth to his own hurt and changeth not.' We have promised the Disciples and we will keep our word. If anyone criticizes our action, you can say that a Yale man made the decision, will not be President another year, and Yale is currently believed to be on the side of the liberals." That was my one action of the year on which I have looked back with satisfaction.

The duties of the office did not prove unduly burdensome. During the autumn, as custom required, I spoke at a number of state conventions. In the most congested week I addressed four—in Illinois, Connecticut, Pennsylvania, and Michigan. Travel was arranged by the national office. Monday morning I met my classes, went by train to New York, and was flown to Chicago and from there to Central Illinois. After my address—in the evening—I was put on a Pullman for Chicago, from Chicago was flown back to New York, took a train to Berlin, Connecticut, was driven to Middletown, spoke at the evening meeting of the Connecticut convention, was driven to a station on the New York Central, took a Pullman to Erie, where I spoke to the Pennsylvania convention, was flown to Detroit by way of Pittsburgh, had a few hours' sleep in a bed in Detroit usually occupied by my host's young son, was driven to Battle Creek, spoke to the Michigan convention, and took a night train for New York. My standard address was on what I believed to be the major mission of Baptists—to preach the Gospel to the poor. I pointed out that Christ made it the climax of the evidence which He gave to the messengers of John the Baptist to demonstrate that He was "the one to come," and that the large majority of Baptists in all lands were from lower economic and social levels. In the winter I presided at a week's sessions of the General Council, which Reuben Nelson, the first General Secretary of the Convention, was endeavoring to use better to coördinate all the boards and their activities.

The final responsibility of my year was to preside at the annual meeting of the Convention. That was held in May and in the auditorium of the Stockyards in Chicago. The meeting was without controversy. Since complaints had been made that recent conventions had not kept to schedule I insisted that we adhere firmly by the time previously announced for addresses, discussions, and action. To set the example and to pacify other participants, at the last minute I shortened the time assigned for the presidential address. To avoid unhappiness over the joint communion with the Disciples—which occupied one evening—at our morning meeting I reminded the Convention of the history of the decisions by which we had committed ourselves to that service. I told them of the differences of opinion among our constituency. I said that as one of our basic Baptist principles we held to the right—and duty—of individual judgment and respect for one another's convictions. I suggested that those who felt we should not hold the service remain away, but not criticize those who went; and that those who went, among whom I announced I would be one, should not criticize those whose consciences kept them away. Since I had no official part in the service, I sat by Hal and Helen Shorrock, Disciples and warm friends, on their way back to Japan after furlough. I am glad to say that, after quiet inquiry, I heard of no criticism of the service or of Baptist participation in it. But the experiment was not repeated and conversations looking toward the union of the two bodies were not continued.

In the 1930's I accepted membership on three other boards. One, in 1937, was the International Committee of the YMCA, through which the Foreign Work, later called World Service, of the Associations of the United States and Canada was administered. For years I had known many of the staff serving abroad, partly because of my connection with the Student YMCA. A major reason for taking on this additional responsibility was to stress the "C" in the YMCA. I had come to fear that the trend was to depart from the centrality of evangelism prominent in the early years of the Foreign Work. A second was the China Medical Board, heavily endowed by the Rockefellers and with its major responsibility the financing of the

Peking Union Medical College. That institution, which sought to bring to the highest standards the emerging modern medical profession in China, had as its foundation a medical school maintained by the united effort of several Protestant mission boards. It sought to be true to that tradition. The Board was not large and I was asked to join as unofficially representing the missionary interests. I soon discovered that our chief function was advisory and that the administration and most of the decisions were by the employed staff in New York. I found the association pleasant and not demanding much time. I served from 1934 to 1949. In the latter year the age of sixty-five, mandatory for retirement of members of boards and staffs of the philanthropic enterprises of the Rockefellers, automatically ended my membership. But each year thereafter I was sent the annual report of the Board. A third membership which I accepted was to the editorial board of *Religion in Life*. *Religion in Life* was a quarterly journal published by the Abingdon Press. The financial responsibility and promotion were Methodist, but the board was drawn from several denominations and the scope of the articles and reviews was ecumenical. Normally the Board met twice a year and the writing obligation was not onerous.

For many years I was a member of the Associated Boards of Christian Colleges in China. However, I was very infrequently in attendance.

The 1940's and 1950's saw the addition of other boards. In 1949, by special request, I became a trustee of the Oberlin in China Association. One or two trips a year to Oberlin were involved. I greatly enjoyed Oberlin and the contacts, but after a few years I came to the conviction that Oberlin had enough expert wisdom without mine and I asked not to be reëlected.

More continuing was the Japan International Christian University Foundation. Largely through the initiative of my friend, Ralph Diffendorfer, then recently retired because of age from long and distinguished service as a secretary of the Methodist Board of Foreign Missions, a dream long cherished in Japan became a reality. A Christian university of the highest academic standards was inaugurated with Japanese trustees and under full Japanese control. Before Japan had fully recovered from the prostration of World War II a substantial sum was collected in that country, chiefly from non-Christians, and a large campus was purchased on the outskirts of Tokyo. Hachiro Yuasa, of whom I have more than once spoken, was elected President. Financial support from the United States was sought through the Japan International Christian University Foundation, with Diffendorfer as President. An ambitious campaign for funds was undertaken, underwritten by the coöperating mission boards. It met with very little concrete success. Diffendorfer resigned. I was on the Foundation representing the American Baptist Foreign Mission Society. Quite unexpectedly, and only a few moments before the meeting to elect Diffendorfer's successor, John Coventry Smith, secretary for Japan of the Presbyterian foreign board, asked me to let my name be presented. Approaches had been made to Joseph W. Grew, recently American Ambassador to Japan, and to a former member of the American consular service in that country, and—not from any lack of interest in the enterprise—both had felt constrained to decline. I told John Smith that in light of other duties I could give very little time, but, if he would do the real work, in view of the very serious emergency which threatened the death of the University before it was born and with great loss to the entire Christian cause in Japan, if he thought my name would be of any use, I would accept. Diffendorfer presided at the meeting, presented his resignation, and I was elected. John Smith was as good as his word. He was continued as Vice-President, succeeded in persuading the mission boards to continue their support, and in other ways met the financial problem. Had he not shouldered the burden, the University would not have been. A few days later Diffen-

dorfer, already suffering from a bad heart, suddenly died.
Year after year at the insistence of the Foundation I was
reëlected and John Smith, as Vice-President and Chairman of the Executive Committee, except in name was
the President. Three times a year I presided at the meetings of the Foundation and appeared at a few other
formal occasions. A major motive in consenting to remain in office was the knowledge of the difficulty of
holding to their original purpose educational institutions
with a professedly Christian objective. The danger of
secularization was especially great in a country, such as
Japan, where Christians were and are a small minority.
If any word of mine would help in warding off the threat
I felt under obligation to say it. I am happy to report that
others more directly in control, both Japanese and non-
Japanese, were keenly aware of the peril and sought to
guard against it. Into its second decade, when these lines
were penned, the University was fulfilling the dream
which had inspired it. It won wide recognition for the
achievement of high scholastic standards, in what had
been an intensely nationalistic country it increasingly became international in student body and faculty, and although it had no requirement of Christian profession for
matriculation or for attendance at chapel or courses in
the faith, the proportion of the student body with Christian commitment increased from freshman through senior year.

In the 1940's I was elected Honorary Pastor of Calvary
Baptist Church in New Haven. When I came on the Yale
faculty I transferred my membership from Granville
where I had been a deacon in the Baptist Church. But, as
I have said, I told successive pastors that I considered my
ministry to be on the Yale campus and could give little
time to the Church. William Lyon Phelps had been the
first Honorary Pastor. After his death I was elected
(1944) to succeed him. My duties were confined to helping the pastor in the monthly communion service and

to occasional preaching. For many years I had a Sunday morning class for Yale students.

As the years passed, I devoted less writing time to East Asia. That was because the numbers majoring in that area were mounting. For that I could claim little or no credit. I had been a trail blazer, but others were moving into that "never, never country." Americans were beginning to realize how important the peoples of the region were for the world, and for the United States in particular. The Japanese invasion of China, which began in 1931 with the creation of Manchukuo and which became full scale in July, 1937, increasingly involved the United States and, with Pearl Harbor, in December, 1941, brought that country into active belligerency. Many who were given a linguistic foundation as part of their training for service with the armed forces or for other government posts utilized it for further specialization.

As I have said, I continued to offer courses in the field, but, to my joy, others were now doing so. My part was still in publication and in teaching, some of the latter on the advanced level. Three books grew out of my writing. Macmillan asked me for a college text which would cover not only China, Japan, and Korea, but also Southeast Asia and India. Since no other book for that purpose existed, I agreed, and *A Short History of the Far East*, of 665 pages, was the result. I dedicated it to William Trufant Foster through whose kindness the course out of which it grew was first offered. Published in 1946, three revisions to bring it up to date were successively made, the last in 1964. It seemed to meet a need, for it and *A History of Christianity* vied with each other in circulations larger than those of any other of my books. In 1946 Harper brought out a much smaller book, *The United States Moves Across the Pacific*. It grew out of a lecture and attempted to show the steps, begun in 1784, soon after it achieved its independence, by which the United States had become increasingly involved in East Asia. *The American Record in the Far East, 1945-1951*, published by Macmillan in 1952, had an interesting history. It was written at the request of the Institute of Pacific Relations. Because its purpose of bettering intelligent international study of what was transpiring on the fringes of the Pacific coincided with one of my concerns, from its beginning I had been a member of that organization, but I had never been active in its affairs. However, it had come under virulent and, I believed, unjust attack by Senator MacCarthy. Although I was already committed to other writing, the subject was timely and important, and I said: "It is time for all good men to rally to the colors." The request was made in the spring of 1951. I asked, as a condition of my acceptance, that the pertinent material be sent to me in Oregon City where I normally spent the summers. Edward C. Carter, the chief promoter of the Institute, had been a casual friend since Student YMCA and Student Volunteer Movement days, but I had not seen much of him for many years, partly, I suspected, because he feared that I would represent missionary conviction in an organization which he was endeavoring to keep religiously neutral. But he was deeply touched by my promise to write the book and made a special trip to New Haven to thank me. The subject was one with which I was already familiar and I had most of the published documents. I wrote the first draft during the month of July, 1951. So far as it had a thesis, it was that the United States could not have prevented the Communist victory on the mainland of China and was in no way responsible for it. That position was highly controversial, but was essentially that of the government of the United States. The Department of State ordered several thousand copies and put many in its centers of information in foreign countries. Senator MacCarthy sent some of his aides to Europe to purge these libraries of books which he deemed dangerous. *The American Record in the Far East* was among them. In the course of a few months, the Department of State restored them to the libraries.

I did not have many students who took their doctorates through the Department of History. Outstanding among the few was M. Searle Bates. A Rhodes scholar, a missionary of the Disciples of Christ, long a teacher of history in the University of Nanking with which his denomination coöperated, through the exigencies of the international situation he was long enough in New Haven to complete the requirements. His dissertation was on a phase of the Han Dynasty, a period in which I had planned to specialize if I had majored in sinology. I rejoiced in his notable contributions in China and in a definitive volume which he wrote on religious liberty. After the Communist occupation of the mainland he returned to this country and became Professor of Missions in Union Theological Seminary in New York. There through a variety of channels he continued to give able, selfless service.

International relations still occupied much of my time. The International Relations Group in New Haven continued through 1946. My course in Christianity and International Relations was offered intermittently. During part of World War II the pacifists of the Yale faculty, most of them in the Divinity School, met regularly for fellowship and to seek to find ways of serving collectively. From time to time I met with groups in the Council on Foreign Relations, chiefly on Far Eastern affairs. I recall especially a small dinner in which John Foster Dulles reported on his negotiation of the treaty of peace with Japan and especially his statement that he believed the odds were about even for keeping Japan out of the Communist ranks. Not many years later at a similar dinner, with Dulles not present, an officer who had been military aide to Dulles and who had been present at the earlier dinner, said that in light of his later visits to Japan he believed the odds were decidedly against Japan becoming Communist.

Much time was taken with conferences and committees on international affairs under the auspices of the

Federal Council and its successor, the National Council
of Churches. Here I had long had happy association with
Walter Van Kirk, who headed that part of the Council's
work and often chaired for him small committees on East
Asian problems. Especially prominent in my memory is
the National Council's wartime Committee for the Study
of the Bases of a Just and Durable Peace. Dulles was the
chairman and gave much time to it. He asked me to serve
as the Far Eastern specialist in a small inner group and
to be the channel of communication on Far Eastern issues between the Committee and the Department of
State. I was glad to act, but am of the opinion that I was
of very little if any use. At the request of Dulles I also
convened smaller subcommittees on Far Eastern problems, among them the future of Korea.

I formed a very high opinion of Dulles, of his intelli-
gence, integrity, and high purpose controlled and inspired by his Christian faith. He was a strong advocate of
the United Nations, when American support for the project was still very uncertain. For some weeks a throm-
bosis in his leg threatened his life. Yet he kept active as
chairman of the Committee and brought the inner group
together in his home. When a crisis arose in the Senate
which threatened the bi-partisan support of America's
endorsement of the United Nations for which Dulles was
working, against his doctor's advice, and knowing that it
might result in his death, he went to Washington and
strove, successfully, to resolve the impasse. He had deep
convictions, but he never attempted to force them on the
Committee. He was tolerant of the pacifist members and
permitted them to present their convictions, although he
said to me privately that he completely disagreed and
believed that professionals in international affairs dis-
missed them as unrealistic. Only once after he became
Secretary of State did I see him. That was at a large
dinner at the Council on Foreign Relations soon after he
had been appointed. He was at the head table and, to
permit my leaving early to catch a train, I was in the

extreme rear. I was deeply touched when he saw me and came the length of the room to shake my hand and to say that he had a copy of *The American Record in the Far East*, but had not yet read it. Roswell Barnes, whom I was honored to number among my close friends from Student YMCA days, a pacifist, a secretary of the National Council of Churches and then of the World Council of Churches, had Dulles's complete confidence and in the latter's last illness Dulles regarded him as his pastor.

As all through the years, students remained my chief interest. I have said something of those who became missionaries. In other ways I cherished friendships with them, both undergraduates and those in the Divinity School. As always, Dwight Hall provided contacts. I came to know well many undergraduates in my classes. In the 1940's I was invited to become a Fellow of Berkeley College. The Yale colleges were begun in the 1930's as small residential units for undergraduates, each with a resident master, a dining hall, a common room, voluntary student organizations, and members of the faculty as Fellows. One purpose was to make possible informal contacts between students and faculty. At the instance of Samuel B. Hemingway, Master of Berkeley, I was assigned to his college. Then began a close and valued friendship with him and his wife. As a collateral descendant of the first student of Yale, he came from an old New Haven family and as a specialist in Shakespeare was a recognized scholar and an excellent teacher. Childless, he and Mrs. Hemingway gave themselves unstintedly to students. Although I was glad of the association with the other Fellows, coming as they did from several departments and schools, I accepted membership in the "fellowship" chiefly as a means of meeting more undergraduates. I was given an office in the college—which, incidentally and to my great pleasure, I shared with Sam Hemingway after he became emeritus. On Monday evenings from seven to eight I was regularly there for any students who cared to come. Counsellees were assigned me, chiefly of my choosing, and I sought them mainly from undergraduates who had a religious interest. Each year I asked an undergraduate to be the informal convener of the Monday night group. Thus, and in other ways, came friendships which continued through the years. Prominent among them were Donald Campbell, James Tanis, and George Anderson. Don was from a plantation on the Arkansas Delta and had been president of the student body in the Little Rock High School. When he entered Yale College a large proportion of the students were veterans returning from World War II, and he felt strange and was very lonely. Early I discerned qualities which I felt fitted him for the ministry. He was undecided vocationally, but had never thought of the ministry. Largely to please me, so he said, to try himself out he gave two summers to serving on the staff of a Little Rock parish. On graduation he entered the Divinity School and for two of his three years was my companion and secretary. Through the years we kept in close touch and I rejoiced in his selfless and courageous ministry as a devoted and wise pastor standing for integration in a state where that was a burning issue. James Tanis came to Yale planning to enter the ministry. In his "bursary" assignment he served in the University Library and was fascinated with it. After graduating from Union Theological Seminary in New York, where he also helped in the library for his scholarship, he was pastor in a New Jersey parish. Later he became librarian of the Harvard Divinity School and showed such initiative and administrative skill that in 1965 he was made head librarian of the entire Yale University library organization. He quietly and firmly held to his Christian faith and in his contacts with individuals proved a real pastor. George Anderson entered Yale with the Lutheran ministry as his objective. Outstanding as a scholar and as a leader, after completing his seminary course at Mt. Airy, where he was president of the student body and had an amazing record as a scholar, he became Professor of Church History in the

Lutheran theological seminary in Columbia, South Carolina, and on his weekends was interim pastor of rural churches or in other ways assisted in neighboring parishes.

Late in the 1940's I was elected to graduate membership in Elihu, one of the senior societies, and availed myself of the opportunity to make friends among successive undergraduate delegations.

As heretofore, my chief contacts were in the Divinity School. Here I continued the informal groups such as I had always had. While working on the *Expansion* volumes, as I have said, I limited them to a single one, of young men headed for foreign missions. After completing the seven volumes I enlarged the groups. To make contact with more men I had two each week. They met by my fireside in my rooms in Stuart House. I also made myself available to Southern Baptists, for many of them found difficult the adjustment to the Yale environment, socially and religiously—in contrast as it was to much of what they had known before coming North.

In the 1940's a new device brought me even closer friendships with students in the Divinity School. Ill health compelled Mrs. Lincoln to ask relief from her weekly appointments for letters. To my joy she was still able to type my books and longer articles. In her place I asked a succession of students to do my letters. The first was James Martin, who was eventually on the staff of the Department of Religion of Denison. The second was Creighton Lacy, of whom I have spoken. Next was Richey Hogg, and with him I devised a new pattern which continued. I asked him not only to take my letters, but as well to be a companion. He occupied a room in Stuart House, at the opposite end from my apartment. We had breakfasts and evening devotions together. In later years especially in asking them to serve I told successive secretaries that I would not attempt to monopolize them; they had their own lives to live and I would never seek to interfere. As I have said, Richey was asked to join me in writing the interpretation of the 1947 Whitby meeting of the International Missionary Council. We attended the conference together and at my suggestion we went to my home in Oregon to write *Tomorrow is Here*. There, without my planning, he met my niece, Wilma Ruth, daughter of my sister Ruth. She was in the University of Oregon Medical School in Portland and was spending her vacation at her home, in a house next to mine. She and Richey were not far from the same age, and after an interval of two or three years were married. Before his marriage, for two years Richey was my secretary. He continued to live in Stuart House and majored with me while a candidate for the B. D. and then for the Ph. D. His doctoral dissertation, *Ecumenical Foundations*, became the definitive history of the origin and early years of the International Missionary Council. We wrote together the official account of the Orphaned Missions Fund. Later he had a short term in India on the faculty of Leonard Theological Seminary and then went on the faculty of Perkins, the divinity school of Southern Methodist University. There in time he became Professor of World Christianity. Among those who followed Richey were "Ned" Steele, of whom I have already spoken, Donald Campbell, Robert C. Johnson, and Rudolf Everest. The last two, like Don Campbell, I had known first as Yale undergraduates.

In the 1940's were several men whom I had first met as undergraduates in Yale College and who came to the Divinity School. I must take the space to mention only three. Two were members of one of the groups which in post-World War II years met by my fireside. Of one, Keith Bridston, I have already spoken. The other, Edward C. ("Pete") Reckard, came to Yale with a letter to me from Frank Price. Therefore I knew him well from his first freshman days. Later he was with the Student Christian Movement of Great Britain and Ireland, then was chaplain of Brown, and eventually pastor of the college church in Claremont, California. The third from Yale

College, Robert S. Bilheimer, never roomed in the Divinity School. To pay expenses he commuted to New York where he served in several secretarial capacities. Among them was executive of the Student Volunteer Movement and later of the Inter-Seminary Movement. Eventually he was for years on the staff of the World Council of Churches. With marked gifts of administration, in each of these organizations he made major contributions. From the World Council of Churches he moved to the pastorate of a Presbyterian church in Rochester, New York, and then to the National Council of Churches.

Because of the inseparable connection with my professional as well as my personal life I must add a word about my Oregon home. There, as I have repeatedly noted, were my rearing and my haven in times of illness. Within its affectionate circle I spent my summer vacations. In their later years I gave much of the vacations to driving my Father and Mother around the countryside. Most was in a Franklin which, blocked up in the winter, was put into active use during the summers and, as it became among the older cars, was a kind of town tradition. Its emergence in June was noted in the local paper. After my Father's death (from a coronary occlusion in 1937) I bought the old home from the executors, subject to my Mother's life occupancy. My Mother lived into her eighty-eighth year and died after a long painful illness. My surviving sister, Dorothy (Mrs. Homer E. Hollowell), for my sister Ruth had died in December, 1941, was unfailingly attentive, and a skilled and devoted nurse was with the patient twenty-four hours a day. As had my Father, my Mother died in the old home. In her later weeks she was much concerned lest her death would leave me without anyone to continue to make the house a home for me. By a fortunate development, in her last hours of consciousness I was able to relieve her mind by telling of an arrangement which seemed to her, and to me, ideal. My Father's youngest half-sister, Freda, was only a few months older than I. We had known each other since childhood, and

were almost like brother and sister. Her husband, John
D. Stewart, was much older than she. For several years
they had lived on her portion of a farm, her childhood
home, which had come to her on the settlement of her
father's estate. There they had specialized in plants and
flowers. John Stewart had reached the age when physical
work was too much of a burden and Freda and he were
planning to sell and move into town. I suggested that on
my Mother's death they make my home theirs. Since the
home was on a half block of land, they could transplant
to it such of their shrubs and lilies as they wished. Here
was a happy solution to their problem and mine. A few
weeks after my Mother's funeral they took possession.
The arrangement proved ideal. John Stewart's declining
strength could be fully occupied with congenial labor.
They were childless. After his death (1961) my aunt
continued to make the house a home for herself throughout the year and for me during the vacations. Summer
time care of the yard gave me the recreation on which I
thrived. Ross Eaton, widower of my sister Ruth, lived
next door. The older son of Dorothy lived across the
street. Dorothy was two blocks away. Therefore Freda
had the congenial family available all the year and I in
the summer. When, in 1961, Dorothy unexpectedly died,
her husband, who had been in charge of my Oregon
business affairs since my Father's death, continued to live
in their home. Therefore during the summers and such
of the other vacations as I spent in Oregon, I was in an
intimate family circle. The "home place" had been built
for my Father in 1891. For me it was filled with memories. Here had been the funeral of my brother Perrin,
who had been drowned in 1903. Here had been many
family fatherings. My Mother's mother died in the room
where my Mother breathed her last. In the next room my
Father died. The weddings of both my sisters had been
before the fireplace around which had centered much of
the life of the family. I was glad to keep the building in
repair and to make physical adjustments in heating,

bathrooms, kitchen, and dining room to take advantage of the conveniences of the changing times. We kept much of the familiar furniture. In the room which had been mine since boyhood I wrote several of such books as did not require an extensive library. For the old home, as for much of life, the only words must be of boundless gratitude.

CHAPTER VIII

THE EMERITUS YEARS

On June 30, 1953, under the Yale rules I became emeritus. By an official act the Yale Corporation added that word to my title. The privileges of the University were still accorded me, but my salary stopped and I was relieved of teaching and administration.

Physically my introduction to the new status was marked by major surgery. For some months I had had increasing discomfort, but Bliss Dayton, whom I consulted, attributed it to the pace I was setting. The preceding year I had carried five courses, as against the normal schedule of three. Two were reading courses but they entailed meeting each class once a week. In addition I was still Director of Graduate Studies in the Department of Religion, I was serving on about thirty boards and committees in New York and New Haven, was seeing *A History of Christianity* through its proof stage, and had given three courses of lectures in other institutions, for which I was writing a small book. But in June a specialist's diagnosis disclosed a diverticulum (rupture) of the bladder, in an advanced stage, a condition which probably had been developing over a number of years. Before the recent advances in surgery this would have meant early and painful death and even then, without antibiotics, also a late development, the chances of recovery and escaping death by infection would have been about five out of ten. An immediate operation was deemed necessary. A great surgeon performed it, no malignancy was

141

found, and I made an excellent recovery. My classmate, John Magee, of whom I have spoken, was retiring as chaplain to Episcopal students at Yale. After the operation, at my request, he laid his hands on me and prayed for my recovery. When I was convalescent, with his unfailing hospitality, Bliss Dayton, who as my physician was in close touch with me, took me to his own home, where he and Mrs. Dayton kept me until sufficient strength had returned to enable me to go to my home in Oregon. By the autumn I was able to return to New Haven and pursue my emeritus schedule.

Only once between June, 1953, and the time when these lines were penned, did illness prove an embarrassment. That was in the summer of 1955. An operation to mend a hernia—by an excellent surgeon in Portland, Oregon—was followed by post-operative pneumonia. Fortunately recovery was prompt and convalescence was in my Oregon home.

Many months before the emeritus status became imminent I had decided how to assign such years as remained. From the experience of older contemporaries in that status, I knew that invitations would come to teach for shorter or longer periods in other institutions. An assured income from annuities, the largest made possible by Yale through the Teacher's Insurance and Annuity Association, meant that the honorarium need not be large. But I had long since decided not to accept appointments which would remove my residence from Yale. Late in my fifties I had faced a similar issue. John Mackay twice asked me to head the Church History Department in Princeton Theological Seminary, of which he was President. I gave the invitation serious consideration, partly because of my friendship with him but chiefly because the post would afford the opportunity to teach the general course in the subject from the global and ecumenical perspective which I was embodying in the seven-volume history of the *Expansion* and from which I was planning to write the text on the history of the faith. I had come to the conviction that to accept would curtail my usefulness. A phrase of Williston Walker, "the gift of continuance," heard long before, rang in my ears. During the few years which remained before the emeritus status I could not hope to make the contribution through Princeton that I could through Yale. In spite of the prejudice aroused by my title and fields, through a variety of channels I seemed to be increasingly accepted at Yale. That would be difficult if not impossible at Princeton, especially since the Seminary and the University did not have the close ties that the Divinity School had with the rest of the University at Yale. The years after reaching the decision had confirmed that judgment.

As I had anticipated, in my emeritus years many invitations came. I recall refusing two in one week, even when I was in my late seventies, and both were to institutions where it would have been a pleasure and an honor to serve.

For my emeritus years I planned two major projects, both outgrowths of long-standing convictions. I would continue to blaze trails in the world mission—a fulfilment of the purpose which I had formed at Gearhart in 1904—and I would give myself to informal contacts and friendships with students.

The trail blazing would be through a five-volume history of Christianity in the nineteenth and twentieth centuries. Because of the global changes issuing from the impact of forces arising in Christendom, I called it *Christianity in a Revolutionary Age*. It was designed to cover the entire world, all aspects of the revolution, and all branches of the faith. Careful inquiry failed to discover any scholar who was planning a similar project. The Yale libraries afforded all the material needed that I would have time to use. To obtain a survey of an aspect of the field in which I had no expert knowledge, before beginning to read extensively I audited a course by Claude Welch, one of my colleagues, on theology since Schleiermacher. I entered into a contract with Harper & Brothers through the ever-generous Eugene Exman. He was dubious about the sale of so large a work and I agreed to waive royalties on each volume until 2,500 copies of the volume had been sold.

To prepare for the project. I undertook a tour of a part of Europe which I had never visited and which entered into the story. That was Scandinavia. In the spring of 1954, I spent several weeks there. That gave me an opportunity to confer with scholars in that area who were specializing on the nineteenth- and twentieth-century history of the Church in their respective countries. By invitation I lectured in the Universities of Copenhagen, Aarhus, Lund, Uppsala, Oslo, and Helsinki. In Helsinki, Arnold Toynbee and I were joint lecturers in a series. We had often met and later I was his guest in London and he mine in New Haven. I found him unfailingly charming, courteous, and stimulating. I was also, but more briefly, in Germany, where I lectured in the theological school at Bethel bei Bielefeld, and met with specialists in the period in which I was interested in Göttingen, Marburg, Heidelberg, and Tübingen. In Louvain the outstanding expert on Roman Catholic theology in the nineteenth and twentieth centuries was very informing. Incidentally, although that had not been a major purpose, I lectured in the Universities of St. Andrews and Glasgow and attended the opening day of the General Assembly of the Church of Scotland. I also had a major address at the annual gathering of the British Congregationalists in Westminster and a few days later was given lunch in the House of Lords by a peer whom I met at that time. Everywhere, especially in Scandinavia, through unfailing courtesy, I was given insights not only into the recent history but as well into the contemporary religious scene. For a companion I took with me George Anderson, who, as I have said, had been a Berkeley College counsellee. As an important and unexpected result of that trip, in Oslo he met the young woman whom he eventually married.

The writing and publication of the five volumes were finished in 1963. In London, as was true of several other of my books and by the initiative of Exman, they bore the imprint of Eyre & Spottiswoode.

In addition to the five volumes, during the first years when they were being written I took on another project, *World Service, A History of the Foreign Work and World Service of the Young Men's Christian Associations of the United States and Canada.* It was undertaken at the request of the Committee on Historical Resources of the North American YMCAs. Because of my long connection with the YMCA I was willing to undertake it, especially since, as I have said, I was familiar with the Foreign Work (latterly World Service) and was a member of the International Committee which supported it. Since I was already committed to the five volumes on *Christianity in a Revolutionary Age,* I made as a condition that the necessary material be sent me to my home in Oregon City where I could give summers to it. The University year I would need to devote to writing on the project for which the Yale libraries were essential. The Committee agreed. I also said that I could not undertake the essential research in the archives, and that someone must be employed who would go through them and select what was pertinent. For that purpose the Committee engaged Mrs. Lennig Sweet. Wife of a YMCA secretary who had served in China, she knew World Service at first hand. She had also aided the author of a larger work on the history of the North American YMCAs and, in addition to being highly competent, was acquainted with many of the details of the story I was to recount. Together we planned the main outlines of the book, and with that to guide her she spent much of three years in bringing the materials together. As a result about half a ton was sent to me, most of it letters and reports mimeographed and in typescript. It occupied part of three rooms on the upper floor of my home. I went through it all. I was greatly aided by E. T. Colton, an older friend of my student days,

who had long served with the Foreign Work and from his
memories and the files compiled a digest of the history of
the New York office through which the funds had been
raised and administered. I was again breaking trail. But,
although World Service involved five continents, the book
compassed a much smaller aspect of the world mission
than I had customarily sought to cover. I assigned three
summers to the project. Two of these were handicapped
by convalescence from surgery and a third was shortened
by a trip to Europe for the Willingen meeting of the
International Missionary Council. I look back on the experience as a kind of nightmare, climaxed by the required condensation to bring the manuscript within the
dimensions set by the Committee and the extensive revision to take advantage of the suggestions of members of
the Committee who read the first and second drafts. The
book was published by the Association Press in 1957.
Later I was glad that I had written it.

In 1962, when *Christianity in a Revolutionary Age* was
behind me, I turned my attention to projects which I had
long been contemplating. One was a thorough revision of
The Chinese: Their History and Culture to take advantage
of the proliferating scholarly output since the second revision and to bring the narrative up to date. I had hoped
that another book might appear which would make revision unnecessary. But Searle Bates from his encyclopedic
familiarity with existing literature in the field reinforced
my judgment that the book served a need as yet unmet. I
gave the larger part of a year to the task and almost
rewrote the second revision. I found myself as excited as
though I was once again blazing trails. In a general way I
had been familiar with what had appeared since the
latest revision, but I now had the opportunity to go
through it more carefully and found it a thrilling adventure—so much had come out. I also gave a revision to *A
Short History of the Far East,* but chiefly to bring the
narrative up to the present and not with a rewriting of

the earlier sections, and to include the latest literature. One of my younger colleagues in the History Department asked me to prepare the China volume on a paperback series which he was editing for survey courses to describe the current situation in a number of countries and to give enough historical background to make the present intelligible. Out of his request came a little book, *China*, published in the autumn of 1964. With one exception the revision of the two earlier books and the writing of *China* constituted the chief contribution of the emeritus years to East Asian studies. The exception was the presidency of the Far Eastern Association in the year 1954-1955. That organization was the outgrowth of the mounting scholarly interest in East Asia. For me election to the office was gratifying recognition of early path-breaking. My presidential address was a survey of the history of American scholarship in the field. During the year of my office steps were taken—not by my initiative but with my hearty endorsement—to broaden the area covered to include Southeast Asia and India. As a result, in 1955 the Far Eastern Association became the Association for Asian Studies. To the joy of those who had watched the development from the days when only a handful were interested, the membership rose to several hundred.

For some years I had been planning a short book which would cover in brief form, hopefully for popular consumption, the history of Christianity and distill my meditation on its place in the total record of mankind seen from the perspective of God's purpose as recorded in the Scriptures. It appeared in January, 1965, as *Christianity through the Ages* and as a paperback to facilitate its sale.

In the spring of 1963, when these writing projects had either been completed or were nearing completion, a quite unexpected invitation came which was to absorb most of my writing time into 1968. The American Bible Society was preparing to celebrate its sesquicentennial, due in 1966. To aid in the commemoration an official history was projected and through Eric M. North I was asked to write it. Eric North had long been the ranking secretary and under his leadership the Society had made amazing strides, and a world organization, the United Bible Societies, had been brought into being to coördinate what was being done in the many countries to put the Scriptures into the hands of the burgeoning millions who as a result of the "literacy explosion" were able to read. He had now retired and planned to devote his energies to make possible the writing of the history. With the approval of the active secretariate, he gathered a small but competent staff to assemble from the prodigious files the material for the history. The invitation came as a thrilling challenge, as a further contribution to the world mission to which I had long been committed, and as requiring the global perspective from which most of my writing had been accomplished. Here, too, was further path-breaking, for no recent comprehensive history of the Society existed and an older one had not been based on substantial research. I quickly accepted. Eric North and his associates went through not only printed material, such as the annual reports and the Society's periodical, but as well and even more important the voluminous correspondence and the manuscript minutes of the Managers and the Managers' committees. They sent the material to me chiefly in the form of bulky essays with references and quotations. Frequent consultations were had and several read my first drafts. We had planned to finish our work in time to have the volume placed on the market at the sesquicentennial (May, 1966), but the material to be covered proved far more extensive than had been anticipated. Now the book is scheduled to appear in 1969.

With the exception of *World Service*, down to the summer of 1964 Mrs. Lincoln had faithfully and faultlessly turned into typescript the first drafts of all the books and many of the articles which I had written since coming on the Yale faculty. Then, because of advancing years and increasing physical weakness, she asked to be relieved of further work. The typing of *The History of the American Bible Society*, therefore, became the responsibility of women engaged by Eric North.

Although I held firmly by my resolution not to accept teaching or other appointments that would involve removing my residence from New Haven, many requests for lectures and addresses came, chiefly from theological seminaries, which could be accepted without unduly interfering with my obligations at Yale. The invitations were from institutions of several denominations, including five with Roman Catholic affiliation. Of the appointments the one requiring the longest absence from New Haven was the Carnahan Lectureship in the Facultad Evangelica Theologia in Buenos Aires in July, 1956. In that institution four denominations coöperated. For the lectures a book was required. It was translated into Spanish as *Desafío a los Protestantes*. The lectures afforded a welcome opportunity to see something of Christianity, especially Protestantism, in South America and, as was true of the Northern European trip of 1953, extensive preliminary correspondence facilitated the use of every day. Taking with me Paul M. Minus as secretary and a friend from his undergraduate years in Berkeley College, and leaving immediately after the Yale Commencement and the fifty-year reunion of my class, I gave a crowded month to the trip, with visits in eight leading cities in five South American countries. That and lecture trips in the United States and Canada, together with one in England and Wales in 1964, were mostly accomplished by air and either during Yale vacations or examination periods when no absence from Yale duties was involved.

Three teaching appointments were accepted which might seem to have entailed exceptions to the decision not to remove my residence from Yale. Fortunately none had that result. The first was to the faculty of Union Theological Seminary in New York City. While Secretary

of the International Missionary Council my friend
Charles Ranson had formulated a plan for bringing
young leaders of the churches of Asia, Africa, the Pacific,
and Latin America for a year of fellowship and study,
thus for a few months relieving them of pressing burdens
and providing opportunity for perspective on their tasks
and enlargement of vision. He had the offer of a large
house in a quiet seaside spot between New Haven and
New York. He asked me, then on the eve of becoming
emeritus, to be resident warden. I declined but said that I
would be willing to do whatever would help which would
not entail leaving Yale. He applied for financial aid to
the Rockefeller Foundation. He was refused on the
ground that such a project should be associated with
some existing educational institution. Henry Pitney
("Pit") Van Dusen, then President of Union, believed the
project too promising to be abandoned and offered to
make it a part of the Seminary's program if the Rockefeller Foundation would underwrite it. He asked me to allow
him to say to the Foundation that I would have some part
in the project if the grant was made. He was a dear
friend of many years and I could scarcely refuse. The
Rockefeller Foundation made a grant of $100,000 and,
whether or not my name influenced the decision, I was
under obligation to keep my word. President Van Dusen
wished me to move to Union and become resident director. That I said I could not do. However, I agreed, if he
wished, to come to New York a day a week and meet the
group. The official name of the project was PARS, the
Program of Advanced Religious Studies. An apartment
house near the Seminary was acquired and was altered to
provide a dining room, a parlor, a chapel, and living
quarters for the Fellows and the resident director and his
family. Ralph Hyslop was appointed director. Searle
Bates, by that time Professor of Missions, gave generously
of his time. The Fellows, as they were called, usually
numbered between twenty-five and thirty. They were
mostly men and were of several communions and coun-

tries. The first year I came on Thursdays during term time and gave a two hour course, followed by discussions and a group dinner. The next few years my responsibilities were limited to Thursdays during the first semester. Since the Rockefeller Foundation declined to renew the subsidy, the budget was altered to enable the original grant to be stretched over nine instead of the five years originally planned, and a generous anonymous gift added a tenth year. In later years because of the financial straits my duties entailed only two two-hour lectures the first semester and attendance at some of the formal functions of the Fellows. At first I groaned inwardly and outwardly over the burden, partly because I thoroughly disliked New York City and the physical setting of Union. But as time passed I was profoundly grateful for the experience and for the contacts with the Fellows and colleagues on the Union faculty. But I never ceased to be glad that I did not have to live in New York.

The spring of 1965, when my appointment as a lecturer at Union expired, a quite unexpected invitation came from the Biblical Seminary in New York City (later New York Theological Seminary) to give a survey course in church history to the entering class. I was to substitute for a man on sabbatical leave. Tuesday and Thursday mornings were entailed, but residence was not required and I could easily make the round trip without absence from my student groups or other obligations at Yale. I was glad to accept, for I could teach church history from the global and ecumenical perspective which was with me a profound conviction.

The third appointment could also be accepted without curtailing Yale duties. It was for two weeks of teaching at the Winona Lake School of Theology. The invitation surprised me, for while I thought of myself as Evangelical and was theologically conservative, Winona Lake was known as a center of the kind of Evangelical conservatism which looked askance at the Ecumenical Movement and, presumably, at Yale. In 1964 I taught four hours a day six days a week for two weeks, the heaviest teaching schedule I had ever carried. Fortunately the subjects, the history of missions and European church history in the nineteenth and twentieth centuries, were among my specialties. The students were from backgrounds quite different from those of students in the Yale Divinity School. Some were as able as any I had ever taught and all of them I enjoyed. Since both courses inevitably included the Ecumenical Movement, I spoke of my happiness in it. A few students felt in conscience bound to tell me that they disagreed, but they were unfailingly courteous. I was even more surprised to be asked to return a second year, 1965. A lighter teaching load was given me, and again in a familiar subject, foreign missions in the nineteenth and twentieth centuries. I was invited, and agreed, to return for a third year, 1966, to give a survey of American church history.

Boards and committees were not as demanding as they had been before I became emeritus. I added none, because of age was not continued on several, and for the same reason begged off from others. I remained on some. For a time I was President of the Yale-in-China Association or, because of the illness of the President, as Vice-President assumed his duties. Eventually, to make room for younger men, I asked to be made an honorary trustee. Similarly, while remaining on the Committee, I was relieved of the chairmanship of the Personnel Committee of Yale-in-China. Year after year the Japanese Christian University Foundation reëlected me President. Usually I attended the semi-annual meetings of the editorial board of *Religion in Life* and the annual Plenary Meetings of the International Committee of the YMCA.

Since it was love of students which had been potent in bringing me into teaching, in my emeritus years I made them, along with writing, my major concern. In the Divinity School three informal groups met weekly by my fireside in my rooms in Stuart House. The only conditions of membership were regular attendance—to insure fellowship. I said to each group that they were to elect their leader and determine their program. Any student was welcome, and in later years a few girls came. Many students I asked personally, partly because I was attracted by them. Some years one of the groups had as a core theological conservatives, including men associated with the Inter-Varsity Christian Fellowship. They would be helped to feel at home on a campus where men of their convictions were a minority and in some of their courses would be exposed to views which troubled them. For a number of years one group was deliberately composed of men who were very uncertain vocationally and religiously. Among them were men who were usually called "Rockefellers." They came on grants from the Rockefeller Brothers given to carefully selected college seniors of more than average ability who had not decided to enter the ministry but were willing to consider it. They could apply to any accredited theological seminary. The majority sought entrance either at Yale or Union. Because they brought an element which augmented the vocational and religious uncertainty which already characterized a substantial minority of the student body, the Yale Divinity School limited the number of "Rockefellers" it would admit in any one year. Membership in a group with others with similar questions helped them to approach their problems together. Other groups were cross sections of the student body. Usually I had not only a fire but apples. Some evenings I took almost no part in the discussions, but I gave priority to the groups and was almost never absent. If a group asked it, and most of them did, I gave them communion twice or three times a year. I cleared a desk, and with the appropriate linen, candles, paten, and chalice made it a communion table. Generally I used the order in the Presbyterian *Book of Common Worship*, based as that was on forms common to many churches for centuries.

Since I ate most of my meals in the Refectory and was usually at chapel and the coffee hour, I was still

looked upon as one of the community of the Divinity
School. To my joy I was called "Uncle Ken" by students
and faculty.

In Berkeley College my status as a Fellow was continued. As earlier, I ate several meals a week in the dining
hall and on Monday evenings from seven to eight was in
my office for all comers. The meals afforded informal
contacts with students and faculty. Almost no Monday
passed without at least one student in my office. Usually
three to six came. Those whom I knew best also con-
formed to the pleasant Yale custom with older men and
called me "Uncle Ken."

During my emeritus years I held membership in the
Elizabethan Club, where in a nineteenth-century house,
comfortably furnished, tea was served afternoons during
term time. Endowed by an alumnus, the club had as its
purpose informal fellowship of students and faculty who
were interested in literature. Since I met there some
whom I seldom saw elsewhere, I made it a custom to
drop in about once a week. Every week or two I looked in
at Elihu, and thus saw undergraduates and recent alumni who were enrolled in the University's professional and
graduate schools.

During most of my emeritus years I continued to teach
a Sunday morning class for students, generally undergraduates, in Calvary Baptist Church.

The custom was continued of having a Divinity School
student as secretary and companion. I engaged them for
only a year at a time, and thus was able to have that kind
of intimacy with more men. Occasionally I asked a man
for a second year.

For an office the Divinity School gave me a three-room
suite. There I did my writing and dictated my letters.
Students and alumni were frequent callers. In these
several ways the kind of friendship with students which
I cherished was multiplied.

The emeritus years passed quickly. They were the richest and happiest of my life. That was partly because of

congenial occupations, partly because of good health, but chiefly because of growing fellowship with God. Wondering and grateful appreciation of the Good News grew. More and more I was aware that God was beyond my full comprehension. Increasingly I came to see that the Trinity is the best description in human language of what underlies and infills the Universe—that the eternal God is Father, Son, and Holy Spirit. Each year I had fresh appreciation of the words of Paul—that now "abide faith, hope, and love, and the greatest of these is love." To me the greatest is love because God is love, and herein is love, not that we loved God but that He loved us and sent His only Son to give us life. Because God is love, we can confidently have faith and hope, both inspired and given by that love. The Spirit Himself bears witness with our spirits that we are children of God, and if children, then heirs, heirs of God and joint heirs with Jesus Christ. What lies beyond this present life I cannot know in detail, but I know Who is there and am convinced that through God's grace, that love which I do not and cannot deserve, eternal life has begun here and now, and eternal life is to know God and Jesus Christ whom He has sent. As I look back across the years I can see how through my long ancestry and through my parents God called me by His grace to reveal His Son in me. Again and again I have betrayed that trust and have been false to that call. I know of a few lives that I have injured. There may have been others of whom I have not been aware. Yet when I have been faithless, He has been faithful. If, as an explorer, I have blazed trails into "the never, never country," if here and there have been lives who have seen, although dimly, His Son in me, that has been through no merit of mine, but because by His initiative God sent His whisper to me.

GENERAL INDEX

157